NEYMAR

MATT AND TOM OLDFIELD

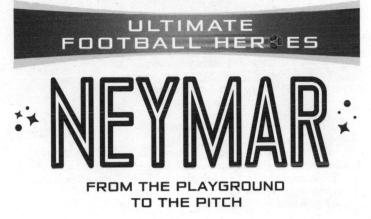

ULTIMATE
FOOTBALL HEROES

NEYMAR

FROM THE PLAYGROUND
TO THE PITCH

DINO

PPublished by Dino Books
an imprint of John Blake Publishing
3 Bramber Court, 2 Bramber Road,
London W14 9PB, England

www.johnblakebooks.com

www.facebook.com/johnblakebooks
twitter.com/jblakebooks

First published in paperback in 2017
This edition published in 2018

ISBN: 978 1 78606 939 9

British Library Cataloguing-in-Publication Data:

A catalogue record for this book is available from the British Library.

Design by www.envydesign.co.uk

Printed and bound in Great Britain by Clays Ltd, St Ives plc

1 3 5 7 9 10 8 6 4 2

Papers used by John Blake Publishing are natural, recyclable products made from
wood grown in sustainable forests. The manufacturing processes conform to the
environmental regulations of the country of origin.

Every attempt has been made to contact the relevant copyright-holders, but some
were unobtainable. We would be grateful if the appropriate people could contact us.

John Blake Publishing is an imprint of Bonnier Publishing
www.bonnierpublishing.co.uk

For Noah and the future Oldfields to come
Looking forward to reading this book together

ULTIMATE
FOOTBALL HEROES

Matt Oldfield is an accomplished writer and the editor-in-chief
of football review site *Of Pitch & Page*. Tom Oldfield is a freelance
sports writer and the author of biographies on Cristiano Ronaldo,
Arsène Wenger and Rafael Nadal.

Cover illustration by Dan Leydon.
To learn more about Dan visit danleydon.com
To purchase his artwork visit etsy.com/shop/footynews
Or just follow him on Twitter @danleydon

TABLE OF CONTENTS

ACKNOWLEDGEMENTS

First of all, I'd like to thank John Blake Publishing –
and particularly my editor James Hodgkinson – for
giving me the opportunity to work on these books
and for supporting me throughout. Writing stories for
the next generation of football fans is both an honour
and a pleasure.

I wouldn't be doing this if it wasn't for Tom. I owe
him so much and I'm very grateful for his belief in
me as an author. I feel like Robin setting out on a
solo career after a great partnership with Batman. I
hope I do him (Tom, not Batman) justice with these
new books.

Next up, I want to thank my friends for keeping

me sane during long hours in front of the laptop. Pang, Will, Mills, Doug, John, Charlie – the laughs and the cups of coffee are always appreciated.

I've already thanked my brother but I'm also very grateful to the rest of my family, especially Melissa, Noah and of course Mum and Dad. To my parents, I owe my biggest passions: football and books. They're a real inspiration for everything I do.

Finally, I couldn't have done this without Iona's encouragement and understanding during long, work-filled weekends. Much love to you.

CHAPTER 1

OLYMPIC GOLD

'We have to win!' Neymar Jr told his teammates. He normally liked to laugh and dance before a match but not this time. He was captain and this was serious. 'Let's get revenge for the 2014 World Cup!'

Neymar Jr was the only member of Brazil's 2016 Olympic squad who had also been there for that awful night in Belo Horizonte two years earlier. When Germany thrashed Brazil 7–1 in the semi-finals on home soil, the whole nation was left heartbroken. Football was their greatest passion.

But it hurt Neymar Jr more than most because he was injured for that game and couldn't be the national hero that they needed. This time, though, as they faced Germany once again, he was fit and raring to go.

'Germany better watch out!' his strike partner, Gabriel Jesus cheered.

After a long season at Barcelona, Neymar Jr had taken a little while to find his form at the Olympics. As the one of the oldest players in the squad, his teammates depended on him. It was a lot of responsibility and after three matches, Neymar Jr hadn't scored a single goal.

'Don't worry,' the coach Rogério Micale told him. 'That was your warm-up; now we need you at your best in these next big games!'

Neymar Jr scored one against Colombia in the quarter-finals, then two against Honduras in the semi-finals. He had rediscovered his *ginga* rhythm, his Brazilian flair, just in time.

'That means you should score a hat-trick in the final!' his teammate Marquinhos joked.

'No pressure, then!' Neymar Jr replied with a smile on his face.

He led the players out on to the pitch to face

Germany at the Maracanã Stadium in Rio de Janeiro. Nearly 60,000 Brazilians had come to cheer on their country, wearing the famous yellow shirt and waving yellow-and-green flags. They were ready for a party, and the noise and colour were incredible.

Neymar Jr stood with his hand on his heart and sang the national anthem loudly. He was so proud to represent his nation and he was one win away from making everyone very happy. He couldn't wait.

Midway through the first half, Brazil won a free-kick just outside the penalty area. It was a perfect opportunity for Neymar Jr. He placed the ball down, stepped back and took a long, deep breath. Then he curled the ball powerfully towards the top corner. It was too quick and high for the goalkeeper to save. The shot hit the underside of the crossbar and bounced down into the back of the net.

Goooooooooooooooaaaaaaaaaaaaaaaaaaalllllllllllllllll lllllllll!!!!!!!!!!!!!!!!!!

Neymar Jr had always dreamed of scoring amazing goals in international finals. Now it was a reality and he would never forget the moment. All of his teammates ran over and jumped on him.

'You did it!' Gabriel shouted.

After the celebrations, Neymar Jr told the others to calm down and focus. 'We haven't won this yet – concentrate!'

Brazil defended well but after sixty minutes, Germany equalised. Neymar Jr had more work to do. He dribbled past one defender and then dropped in a clever Cruyff Turn to wrong-foot a second. It was magical skill and the crowd loved it. He now had the space to shoot. The ball swerved past the goalkeeper's outstretched arm but just wide of the post.

'So close!' Neymar Jr said to himself, putting his hands on his head.

Brazil attacked again and again but they couldn't find a winning goal, even after thirty minutes of extra-time. Now it would go to penalties.

'I'll take the last one,' Neymar Jr told Micale. He was determined to be the national hero this time.

After eight penalties, it was 4–4. When Brazil's goalkeeper Weverton saved the ninth spot-kick,

Neymar Jr had his golden chance. He walked from the halfway line towards the penalty spot with thousands of fans cheering his name.

He picked up the ball, kissed it and put it back down. As he waited for the referee's whistle, he tried to slow his heartbeat. If he was too excited, he might kick it over the bar. He needed to be his normal, cool self.

As he ran up, he slowed down to try to make the German goalkeeper move early. The keeper dived low to the right and Neymar Jr put his shot high and to the left. As the ball went in, Neymar burst into tears of joy. He had led his country all the way to the Olympic Gold Medal for the first time ever. As he fell to his knees and thanked God, the other Brazil players ran to hug their hero.

'You always said that we could do it!' his teammate Luan shouted. 'Now it's carnival time!'

As Neymar Jr got back on his feet, he listened to the incredible noise of the Maracanã crowd. It was the best thing he had ever heard.

'Imagine what the atmosphere would have been

like if we'd made it to the World Cup final and won it in 2014!' Neymar Jr thought to himself, but it was time to forget about the pains of the past and move forward. Thanks to him, his country was back at the top of world football again.

'Thank you!' the coach Micale said to him, giving him the biggest hug of all.

He was still only twenty-four but Neymar Jr had already been Brazil's number one superstar for years. There was so much pressure on him but he refused to let his country down, even after moving to Spain to play for Barcelona.

Neymar Jr had Brazil to thank for everything: the love of his family and friends; the support of his coaches at Portuguesa Santista and Santos; and above all, the amazing skills that he had first developed in street football, beach football and *futsal* matches in São Paulo.

CHAPTER 2

A LUCKY ESCAPE

'Nadine, don't forget Junior's blanket!' Neymar
Senior called into the house. They were driving to
Santos to visit some relatives and they needed to
keep their newborn son warm. In his baby seat,
Neymar Jr giggled and wiggled his toes.

'I'm still not sure about that name,' Nadine
muttered as she wrapped the blanket tightly around
her son. She still hadn't forgiven her husband. 'Why
didn't you just go with Mateus like I asked you to? I
thought you liked that name too! It's much nicer.'

'You'll learn to love this name, I promise!' Neymar
Sr replied. Like father, like son.

As he got into the car, he groaned. Neymar Sr's

body hurt more and more after every match that he played for União FC in the third division of the São Paulo league. He was getting older and now that he had a child to look after, he was always tired. Football was the first love of his life and he worked hard to earn enough money for his family. But perhaps his dad, Ilzemar, was right. Was it time to finally give up on his dream and find a proper job with a better wage?

In the passenger seat, Nadine turned to check on her little boy – he was fast asleep. 'He looks so peaceful,' she said lovingly. 'Please drive carefully! The roads are wet today.'

The journey down the mountain from Mogi das Cruzes was always dangerous. The roads were narrow and winding, with blind bends everywhere. Also, Brazilians weren't known as the safest drivers in the world. Neymar Sr wasn't going to take any risks with their tiny and precious new arrival.

But as they turned a corner, a car came towards them at high speed. 'Watch out!' Nadine shouted. Neymar Sr swerved to the left to try to avoid it but there wasn't enough time. There was a loud crashing sound and then everything went black for a minute. Once the shock had worn off, the pain was unbearable.

'Nadine, are you okay?' Neymar Sr called out. It felt like he had broken every bone in his body.

'Yes,' she managed to reply eventually. 'But what about Junior?'

Slowly, they turned around to look – the back seat was empty. 'Where is he?!' Nadine shouted, panicking.

Neymar Sr tried to stay calm but the possibilities were terrible. The car was right on the edge of a cliff – what if their son had been thrown out of the car? He prayed to God to protect Neymar Jr. When he tried to escape from the car to check, he couldn't move.

'We're going to get you both out of there!' a voice shouted from outside. Fortunately, people who had seen the accident had stopped to help them.

'Our son was in the car too but we can't find him!' Neymar Sr cried out.

The helpers forced the back door open and soon

there was very good news. 'He's here!' someone cheered. Neymar Jr had fallen into the footwell under the front seat.

'Is he alive?' Nadine asked, fearing the answer. If they had all survived the crash, it would be a miracle.

'Yes!' a woman replied, showing her the baby in her arms. He had some cuts and bruises but his eyes were open and Neymar Jr began to cry. Tears of relief rolled down Nadine's cheeks. She was so happy to see her son's little face.

'What about my husband?' she asked next.

The ambulance rushed Neymar Sr straight to the hospital. His injuries were very serious and it took a long time for them to heal. When Neymar Jr came to visit, with a small bandage tied around his head, and saw his dad surrounded by all the big medical machines, he burst into tears.

'Don't worry, Junior – I'm just lucky to be alive!' Neymar Sr reassured him, holding his hand. 'I'll be better soon and then we'll able to play together again.'

When Neymar Jr was one year old, his dad was finally able to hold him in his arms again. It was a beautiful moment after so many months of waiting.

'My golden child,' Neymar Sr said, kissing his son's forehead. 'You're going to grow up and do something very special – I'm sure of it!'

As one football career faded out, another was about to begin.

CHAPTER 3

RUNNING AROUND

'Junior, please sit still for one minute!' Nadine begged. She was trying to feed him but he preferred to be moving at all times, and kept wriggling around in his chair. 'Fine,' she said, 'once you've had a few more vegetables, you can go back to your games!'

Neymar Jr was only three years old, and so too young to go out playing in the neighbourhood with the other local boys. For now, their house had to be his playground. He climbed all over the furniture and ran from room to room, knocking into anything that got in his way.

'Careful, Junior!' his dad shouted. 'We can't afford to replace all the things that you break.'

Neymar Sr was working three jobs at the
same time but it wasn't making them rich at all.
Sometimes they couldn't pay the electricity bill and
so the family had to live by candlelight. In the semi-
darkness, Neymar Jr's running around was even
more dangerous.

'What are we going to do?' Nadine asked her
husband. She was pregnant again and they needed to
think about the future of their family.

'We'll have to move in with my parents for now,'
Neymar Sr replied. 'It's not perfect but we can save
up money for a home of our own.'

In his grandparents' house, Neymar Jr shared a
bedroom with his parents and soon with his baby
sister Rafaela too. It was very cramped but that didn't
stop the young boy's games. He only needed a tiny
bit of space and his imagination.

'We're under attack!' he shouted. 'Go Go Power
Rangers, it's time to fight back!'

Neymar Jr's games changed when he was given his
first football. Suddenly, it was his favourite toy and
he took it everywhere with him. When his parents

were in the kitchen, Neymar Jr turned the bedroom
into an obstacle course. He started at the door and
dribbled as fast as he could between the mattress and
the wardrobe. When Rafaela and his cousins were
around, he made them play too.

'Leave us alone – we're playing our own game!'
his sister complained.

'You don't have to do anything – just stand still,'
he told her. 'You're the goalpost!'

Sometimes Neymar Jr was the striker. He dribbled
around one cousin and then another before kicking
his little football as hard as he could. As it flew
between Rafaela and another cousin, he celebrated
wildly with his shirt over his head.

'And Neymarzinho scores another brilliant goal!'

Sometimes he was the goalkeeper, making
incredible saves by diving across the mattress. And
sometimes he just practised his technique, kicking
the ball against the wall again and again, first with
his right foot and then with his left foot.

Neymar Sr was very pleased with his son's
progress. When he passed him the ball, he didn't

pick it up and run away with it like most toddlers. Instead, he kicked it straight back with a strong and accurate pass. Neymar Jr's little face looked so serious.

'He's going to be a top footballer – I know it already!' Neymar Sr told his wife excitedly.

But Nadine wasn't so impressed. 'Junior's got too much energy to be stuck in here all day,' she said. 'If he breaks one more vase, I'm going to scream!'

'Okay, I'll take him to my beach football match this weekend,' Neymar Sr told her. 'He can run around while I play and people will keep an eye on him. I'll make sure he's exhausted by the time we come back!'

Neymar Jr loved being outside in the sunshine but the football match was really boring to watch. His dad had made him leave his football in the car and so he switched to Plan B: running *without* the ball. There weren't many spectators in the stand and so Neymar Jr could run up and down the big steps and then along each row. There was plenty of space for adventures.

Amongst the spectators was Betinho, a local youth coach and scout. He had brought his young son along to watch the game but, like Neymar Jr, the boy quickly got bored and went off to explore.

'Where is my son? I must keep an eye on him!' Betinho remembered when the game stopped because of an injury. As he turned and looked across the stand, he spotted another skinny little boy running around.

'He's got a nice style,' Betinho said to himself. He had been scouting young footballers for years and so he knew exactly what to look for. Skilful Brazilians moved in a special, natural way that combined balance with agility and rhythm. They looked like they were dancing as they dribbled past defenders.

'I'd like to see that kid running with a football!' Betinho thought. So he asked a friend, 'Who is that boy?'

'That's Junior, son of Neymar Sr,' the friend replied, pointing down at the winger on the pitch.

When the match finished, Betinho went to speak to the boy's dad. 'Well played today. I saw your son

up in the crowd. Is he playing for a team yet?'
he asked.

'Not yet,' Neymar Sr replied. 'He's still only five years old. Isn't that too young?'

'You're never too young to start playing football!' Betinho argued with a smile on his face. 'Can I please train your son? He'll love it and you never know – we might have a world champion right here!'

CHAPTER 4

FUTSAL VS STREET FOOTBALL

'Here you go,' Betinho said, passing a football to Neymar Jr. 'Let's see if I was right about you!'

Neymar Jr controlled it with his left foot, flicked it to his right foot and then passed it back. He hadn't done anything particularly special yet but Betinho was already excited. Eight years earlier, he had discovered a brilliant young player called Robinho and he was getting that special feeling again.

'Okay, let's see you dribble. Try to get past me!'

Neymar Jr ran forward at speed – this was his favourite game. As he got near to Betinho, he pretended to go left but did a step over and went right.

The youth coach was too amazed to move. 'Wow, yes you've got *ginga!*'

Neymar Jr looked confused. 'What's that?'

'It's Brazilian flair,' Betinho explained. 'You can't teach *ginga* – it's a natural style that makes us the best footballers in the world! Do you like dancing to samba music?'

Neymar Jr nodded.

'I thought so! It's the same thing really – when you take that rhythm and movement and you put it on the football pitch, it's magical!'

Betinho took his new star for a trial at Clube de Regatas Tumiaru, the local *futsal* club where he coached. *Futsal* was a five-a-side indoor sport that many young Brazilians played before moving on to football. The ball was smaller and heavier and the hard court wasn't so large, so players needed great close control and clever skills.

'We know that you've got the technique but it's time for you to learn about the other areas of the game,' Betinho told Neymar Jr beforehand. 'Things like teamwork, stamina, strength and tactics are just as important.'

Neymar Jr listened to every word of advice because he wanted to get better and better. In the passing and dribbling practices, he was focused and precise. He didn't do anything wrong but nor did he do anything exceptional. He was saving that for the match at the end.

When the coach blew the whistle to start, all of Neymar Jr's teammates chased after the ball. It was chaos in the middle of the court as nine kids battled each other.

'I'm in space!' Neymar Jr called from out on the wing.

When his team won possession, they passed to him, and he dribbled forward and scored easily.

'I've been trying to get them to spread out like that for months!' one of the other coaches said with a smile. 'He's a smart kid.'

'I didn't even tell him to do that,' Betinho replied. 'He's a thinker!'

As his opponents passed the ball to each other,

Neymar Jr was already running to where he thought
their next pass might go. And once he won the ball
back, he never lost it. He dribbled whenever he
could but if he couldn't, he made sure that he gave it
to his teammates.

'Excellent, Junior!' the coach shouted, clapping
loudly.

The other team soon realised how good Neymar
Jr was and they tried to double-mark him. But he
hypnotised them with his quick feet every time.

'I've never seen a kid that good,' the other coach
admitted.

'Robinho was very good but I think Junior might
be even better!' Betinho predicted.

When the session finished, the boys got changed
and left, one by one, until only one remained:
Neymar Jr.

'Come on, your dad will be waiting for you at
home,' Betinho called to the boy but he was in his
own world, gliding past imaginary defenders and
shooting past an imaginary goalkeeper. 'The goal will
still be here next time, I promise!'

Neymar Jr took one last shot and followed Betinho to the car. He was pleased with his first practice. There was still a lot of work to do but it felt good to play for a proper club.

'How was it?' his dad asked him as he ran inside for dinner.

'Awesome!' he replied with a huge grin on his face.

'That kid might be a football genius one day!' Betinho had told Neymar Sr as they said goodbye.

From that first day onwards, Neymar Jr was the star of the team. He scored lots of great goals as Tumiaru won every local tournament and trophy. The club were so desperate to keep him that they started sending food baskets to his house.

'Good boy, you're already earning a wage for the family!' Neymar Sr joked.

Betinho's only problem was actually finding his protégé. Neymar Jr was always playing football but where? As soon as school finished each day, he rushed outside to play football with his friends. The streets were always full of cars and bikes but they used whatever space they could find.

Neymar Jr loved the noisy atmosphere: the people chatting, the car horns sounding, the Brazilian hip-hop music blaring. It gave him the extra energy he needed to show off his full range of tricks and flicks. That was what street football was all about. They often played barefoot with a deflated ball and the contest was simple: who could do the coolest bit of skill?

'Is Junior at home?' Betinho asked, when he came to pick Neymar Jr up for training at Tumiaru.

Nadine shook her head. 'No, sorry, he's still out playing.'

Betinho drove slowly through the streets looking for him. Eventually, he spotted Neymar Jr. A crowd of people were standing around, cheering loudly as the others tried to get the ball off him. He was a born entertainer.

'Junior!' Betinho shouted through the car window. 'Come on, you're late!'

Neymar Jr rolled the ball off his neck and back down on to his foot. Then he flicked it up into his arms and sprinted to the car.

'I'll be back after training!' he called to his friends.

CHAPTER 5

ON THE BEACH

'That's it!' Neymar Sr encouraged his son. It was a
very warm afternoon in São Paulo and for once, he
had a day off from work. That meant only one thing:
football practice. 'And if you want to kick it really
hard, use the top of your foot. Yes, just like that!'

As the football flew through the air, Neymar Jr
chased after it across the hot sand. If it went in
the sea, the ball might drift away. That would be
a disaster.

'Don't step on a jellyfish!' his dad joked.

Neymar Sr had built a new home for his family
in Praia Grande, an area with a long coastline
of beautiful beaches. In the evenings and at the

weekends, thousands of Brazilians came down there to play volleyball and football.

'If you can play well here,' he told his son, 'you'll be unbelievable on the pitch at Santos!'

Neymar Jr loved playing beach football because it was a real test of his technique. He also played *futsal* but he preferred playing outside with the sun, sea and sand.

'Slow down, Junior – you don't want to injure yourself!'

Balance was very important in beach football because the surface wasn't smooth and flat like grass. It was lumpy and covered in obstacles like shells and litter. If you took one wrong step, you could easily twist your ankle. Luckily, Neymar Jr was a natural, just like Betinho had predicted.

Neymar Jr could dribble really fast with either foot and he could shift his body to either side in an instant to escape a tackle. He was only seven years old, and yet Neymar Sr was already finding it difficult to get the ball off him.

'You dance like a Brazilian!' his dad laughed.

Thanks to all the hours spent practising in the bedroom at his grandparents' house, Neymar Jr didn't panic when there wasn't much space around him. Instead, he was calm and creative, and improvised something special.

'Yes, you're certainly going to be a star one day!' his dad told him.

But Neymar Jr was impatient. He was ready for the next challenge – trying out his skills in proper beach football matches. That was the best way to keep learning.

'Dad, can we ask to join in?' he said, pointing to the people playing nearby.

Neymar Sr was worried. There were a few kids playing in the game but none were as young and skinny as his son. What if he got badly hurt? Some of the adults looked very strong but at least he would be there to protect Neymar Jr.

'Okay, but first I need to give you two more lessons,' he said.

His son rolled his eyes. 'Not more lessons – I want to *play!*'

Neymar Sr ignored him. 'Lesson One: Don't be a show-off. If you're going to dribble with the ball, do it to create a goal. If you try to do lots of tricks and don't pass the ball, your teammates will be angry and your opponents will tackle you even harder.'

His son nodded.

'And Lesson Two: Work hard. Always keep moving to find space away from the defenders. Make life difficult for them. When you stand still, it's easy to mark you.'

Neymar Jr nodded again. 'Now can we play?'

At first, Neymar Sr felt nervous every time his son touched the ball. But soon, he relaxed and enjoyed himself because Neymar Jr was playing very well. He had listened carefully to all of his dad's advice. He ran and ran to help his team and when they attacked, he was fearless against players twice his size. He dribbled down the wing and if he couldn't get past the defender, he looked up for the pass, rather than being selfish.

'Wow, your son is brilliant,' one of the adults said to Neymar Sr. 'His ball skills are better than mine!'

'Thanks,' he replied proudly. And to himself, he muttered, 'He's got two good coaches!'

Neymar Jr's team won and as father and son walked home together, the boy talked happily about the match.

'Did you see it when I flicked it round the fat guy and then crossed the ball for Jorge to score?'

His dad nodded.

'Did you see the tackle I did on the midfielder? I was so quick that he didn't even see me coming!'

His dad nodded.

'And did you see the goal I scored at the end? The goalkeeper didn't think I had the power to kick it that hard!'

Neymar Sr smiled; he could remember being just as excited about football when he was younger. 'Junior, of course I saw it – I was playing in the match too!'

Neymar Jr couldn't wait to share his stories with Nadine and Rafaela at dinner.

'Mum, I had so much fun!' he began, wolfing down the rice and beans on his plate. Twenty minutes later, he was only halfway through his story of the match.

'This is so boring!' Rafaela moaned, pretending to yawn.

'Yes, can we skip to the end now please?' Nadine asked nicely. 'Otherwise, we might be here all night! Did you win?'

'Of course!' Neymar Jr cheered with a mouth full of food.

'That's disgusting!' Rafaela said, but they all laughed.

When Neymar Sr went to say goodnight to his son, he was lying in bed surrounded by round objects. There was barely room for his little body. Some kids slept with animal soft toys next to them, but Neymar Jr chose footballs.

'Well played today,' Neymar Sr said, kissing him on the forehead. 'We'll work on a few more things next weekend – there's always room for improvement!'

CHAPTER 6

GREAT TIMES AT GREMETAL

'I've got a new coaching job at Gremetal,' Betinho told Neymar Sr one day, 'and I really want Junior to come with me. What do you think?'

'I think it's a very good idea,' Neymar Sr replied immediately. He trusted Betinho with his son's future and he knew that Gremetal was a great *futsal* club that looked after its young players.

'Great to see you!' Luiz Ricardo shouted, giving Neymar Jr a high-five. They knew each other well from their street football games in Praia Grande. 'Guys, this is Junior. Just wait until you see him play – he's incredible. We're going to win everything now that he's here!'

Luiz was right. Once Neymar Jr arrived, the Gremetal Under-11s were unbeatable. He was their youngest player but he was so brilliant that he quickly became one of the leaders. He even made matching white headbands for his teammates.

'We all look like Karate Kids now!' he laughed.

The other players were good but Neymar Jr was in a league of his own. He started every attack and he was there at the end too, either with a shot or a cross. Despite all his skills, he wasn't a selfish player. As long the team won, he didn't mind who scored.

'We win together!' Gremetal cheered before each match.

As Neymar Jr ran towards goal, defenders knew what was going to happen but there was nothing that they could do to stop it. Even fouling didn't work because they couldn't get close enough to kick him. He was just too quick, too skilful, too clever – too good. Betinho's job was easy and his instructions were simple: 'Just play your natural game'.

Neymar Jr was the king of the *futsal* court and as

he got older, more and more scouts came to watch him play.

'Please don't leave us, Junior!' Luiz said as the team relaxed after yet another victory. They were enjoying their success and they didn't want it to end.

Neymar Jr smiled. 'Don't be silly, the only place I'm going to is Dudu's house!'

Dudu, Luiz, Michael and Neymar Jr usually spent their whole weekends together. They worked hard and they played hard too. When they weren't playing football together for Gremetal, they were often playing football against each other in the street. The two-vs-two matches were very competitive.

'Okay, I'm playing with Junior this time,' Luiz said before anyone else could beat him to it. 'It's my turn!'

Whoever played with Neymar Jr almost always won; it was as simple as that. After about thirty seconds, Dudu and Michael stopped marking Luiz and both focused on the danger boy.

'Michael, if you tackle him from the left, I'll tackle him from the right,' Dudu suggested. 'Don't let him escape!'

But Neymar Jr spun around on the ball, did a couple of step overs and played a perfect pass to Luiz. 1–0!

Fifteen minutes later, it was 3–3. 'Next goal wins!' Luiz shouted.

Neymar Jr shielded the ball from Dudu and looked for a path to goal. He rolled the ball from right to left, as if to pass to Luiz. As Michael ran to block it, Neymar Jr flicked the ball behind him instead and tried to turn. Dudu stuck out his leg and tripped him up.

'Foul!' Luiz shouted. 'You can't do that!'

Dudu shrugged dramatically like the professionals. 'I didn't touch him – he just fell!'

As the others fought over whether it was a penalty or not, Neymar Jr got up and wiped his bleeding knee. He had an idea.

'Okay, if I can kick the ball from here into that bin over there, we win. If I can't, we keep playing.'

Michael nodded. 'That sounds fair, but you only get one go!'

The bin was at least twenty yards away but

Neymar Jr had been practising his long-range passing. This was the ultimate test. He chipped the ball carefully and it floated through the air. He'd got the distance just right but would it land neatly inside or bounce off the edge? The ball rolled around the rim and dropped in.

'Yes!' Luiz shouted, giving Neymar Jr a big hug. 'That was amazing!'

Michael was disappointed to lose but he patted his opponent on the back. 'I've got no idea how you do stuff like that. I'm just glad you're on my team for Gremetal!'

'What time do you guys have to be home?' Dudu asked. 'Have we got time for a quick game of FIFA?'

There was always time to play PlayStation. They had changed the names of four top players so that 'Junior', 'Dudu', 'Michael' and 'Luiz' were teammates for the Brazilian national team. Neymar Jr was allowed to be his hero – the best player in the world, Ronaldo.

'It's only fair,' Dudu had decided after listening to the arguments. 'Junior is the best player here!'

Ronaldo was a striker at Italian club Inter Milan and Neymar Jr loved to watch him glide past defenders to score great goals. He was always looking for new tricks to learn. The boys took it in turns to lead their nation to 2002 World Cup glory.

'How amazing would it be if this was real life?' Luiz said as they watched the players lift the golden trophy. 'Imagine how cool it would be to play for Brazil!'

For most of them, that was just a fantasy. But for Neymar Jr, it was a genuine possibility. He was still only eleven but everyone agreed that he had the talent to reach the very top. The next step would be moving from *futsal* to association football.

CHAPTER 7

SCOUTED BY SANTOS

Zito had been keeping an eye on Neymar Jr for a while. As a Santos FC legend with over fifty caps for Brazil, he was a well-informed man. If there was a great young player in São Paulo, he knew about him. He had first heard the name 'Neymar Jr' from Alemão, a massive Santos supporter who ran a bar near the Vila Belmiro Stadium.

'I think you'll really like him,' Alemão told him with a smile. 'He plays *futsal* for Gremetal and he's got unbelievable talent for an eleven-year-old!'

When Zito asked one of the other Santos youth coaches if he had heard of Neymar Jr, he laughed. 'Oh yes! Gremetal thrashed our Under-12s 9–0 two weeks ago. That kid scored a hat-trick and set up most of the other goals too. He's special, that's for sure!'

'Do you know if he's playing association football for a club?' Zito asked.

'He's at Portuguesa Santista, I think.'

As Zito waited for the Santista match to begin, he watched Neymar Jr warming up. He was laughing with his teammates, while doing keepy-uppies at the same time. He made it look as easy as walking. The kid's height wasn't a problem but he did look far too skinny.

'There can't be any muscle on his body at all,' the Santos youth coach thought to himself. 'A gust of wind might blow him over!'

But once the game kicked off, Zito saw that it didn't really matter. Neymar Jr's dribbling skills made it almost impossible for anyone to get near enough to push him around. Everything about him was so quick: his feet, his change of direction, and his football brain.

He was the best player on the pitch by miles. As soon as the ball came to him, space seemed to open up in front of him like magic. He sprinted forward, nutmegged one defender, played a one-two with a teammate and then hit a fierce shot into the bottom corner.

Goooooooooooooaaaaaaaaaaaaaaaaaaaaalllllllllllllllllll llllllllll!!!!!!!!!!!!!!!!!!!!!!!!!!

'We have to sign him!' Zito shouted out loud. He was on his own but he didn't care if he sounded crazy; he had never been so excited about a youngster before. He looked around to see if any other local scouts were watching. Surely Santos couldn't be the only club chasing this wonderkid?

That same day, Zito marched into the office of the club chairman, Marcelo Teixeira. 'I'm sorry to disturb you but I've just found a superstar and we have to act fast before another team gets him!'

Teixera was shocked. 'Wow, I've never seen you like this. The kid must be amazing – sure, go get him!'

Neymar Jr couldn't believe it when he heard the news. His dream was coming true. He would be following in his dad's footsteps: first Portuguesa Santista and now Santos.

'Are you absolutely certain that they've got the right player?' he asked his dad. His Gremetal strike partner, Léo Dentinho, was also very highly-rated. Maybe the club had mixed the two of them up.

'Son, they're desperate to sign you!' Neymar Sr told him proudly. 'They're offering a five-year contract with a salary.'

Neymar Jr smiled. 'Now I'll really be earning a wage for the family!'

Nadine laughed. 'Yes, but you know you won't just be playing football all day every day, don't you? You'll still be going to school – education is important too.'

As the family celebrated at dinner, a horrible thought crossed Neymar Jr's mind.

'Dad, what about Betinho? Is he coming too?'

He really didn't want to leave his coach behind. What would he do without him after so many years of success together?

'I'm not sure, Junior,' his dad replied, looking sad. 'I'll speak to Santos but I'm afraid he may have to stay with Santista.'

Fortunately, Neymar Sr was brilliant at negotiating and a few days later, he had great news for his son. 'Betinho is going with you! I told them that the deal was off unless they signed your coach too. And they agreed!'

Neymar Jr was delighted. With his dad and Betinho at his side, offering support and advice, he truly believed that he could fulfil his great potential. This was his big chance to develop into a top professional footballer and, hopefully, a Brazilian international. He was ready to make the most of the opportunity.

He went to Gremetal to say goodbye to his teammates. He would really miss them.

'Don't worry, we're going with you,' Dudu said, after listening to his friend's farewell speech. 'Apparently, you weren't enough; they wanted all of us!'

It was more good news for Neymar Jr. 'Santos, here we come!' they all cheered together.

As he arrived at the Meninos da Vila training centre, Neymar Jr was buzzing. There were skilful youngsters everywhere, playing on perfect green pitches in white and black shirts. He was one of them now – a Santos footballer, just like Brazil's greatest ever player, Pelé.

'I'm going to be very happy here!' Neymar Jr said to himself. He couldn't wait to get started.

CHAPTER 8

FINDING SPACE TO SHINE

'No way!' Zito said, shaking his head. 'Junior's not strong enough to play eleven-a-side football for you yet. He's only just arrived at the club. Maybe next year, when he's developed more muscle.'

But Lima, the Santos Under-15s coach, wasn't going to give up. He had seen Neymar Jr's talents on the *futsal* court. He was exactly the kind of exciting player that his team needed. 'He's far too good to be playing with your Under-13s!' he argued. 'He needs a bigger challenge. At least let him come and train with us. I promise he won't play a match until you think he's ready.'

In the end, Zito lost the fight and Neymar Jr joined

the Under-15s. He was the smallest and youngest player in the team but that never scared him. His dad and Betinho had taught him well. He understood that he had to keep testing himself if he wanted to become a Brazilian hero.

'I've played against older kids all my life!' Neymar Jr told Lima with a confident smile on his face.

That smile didn't last long, however. Under-15s football was much tougher than Neymar Jr had expected. The problem was that some of his opponents were far too old for the age group.

'That kid looks closer to thirty than fifteen!' Betinho shouted as a huge defender barged into the back of Neymar Jr. The skinny thirteen-year-old went flying to the floor. 'Referee, I'd like to see his date of birth please!'

'It's ridiculous,' Neymar Sr said angrily. 'They're fouling him every time. He's got no space to shine.'

Every week, Neymar Jr left the pitch covered in cuts and bruises but he never gave up. Instead, he just worked even harder in training.

'Come on, it's time to go home!' Lima shouted. It was dinner time and he was hungry.

'Just five more shots!' Neymar Jr replied.

His coach sighed; it was the same old story. 'Why are you hitting them all with your right foot?' he asked.

'My right foot is much more powerful than my left.'

'That's not a good reason!' Lima said. 'The best players can shoot with both feet and that makes it much more difficult for defenders to stop them. If you practise, you can make your left foot just as powerful. Not now, though. It's time to go home!'

Neymar Jr was improving every day in training but for the first time ever, he wasn't enjoying the weekend football matches.

'Are you okay, son?' Neymar Sr asked as they drove home from a game.

Neymar Jr nodded slowly. 'I can play so much better than that but I don't know what to do against those giants. They don't even care about the ball – they just want to hurt me!'

They needed to find a solution to the problem. A talent like Neymar Jr's could not be wasted.

'Do you think he should go back to the Under-13s?' Betinho asked. 'Perhaps he needs to play with kids his own age for a bit longer.'

Lima thought for a few minutes. Suddenly, he banged the desk with his fist. 'No, I've got a better idea!'

At the next training session, the coach spoke to his young attacker. 'How are your ankles after the last game?'

Neymar Jr looked down and shrugged. 'They're fine, thanks.'

'For next week's match, we're going to make a change,' Lima explained. 'This time, you won't be playing as the centre forward.'

Neymar Jr looked very upset. 'I know I haven't been scoring enough goals but please don't–'

His coach interrupted him. 'No, I'm not putting you on the bench! I want you to play as the playmaker instead, in between the midfield and the strikers. At the moment, you're too close to the defence to use your skills and speed. They're much stronger than you

and so they push you around. Let's see what you can
do with a bit more space to dribble!'

The youngster nodded. He was relieved to hear
that he was still in the team and he liked the sound
of his new role.

Neymar Jr got the ball just inside the opposition
half. One of the defenders rushed out to tackle him
but Neymar Jr had time to turn and flick the ball past
him. He sprinted towards goal. The other centre-
back tried to stop him but Neymar Jr did one step
over and then another, and then another. Which way
would he go? The defender tried to keep his eyes on
the ball, rather than the magical, dancing feet, but it
was impossible. Neymar Jr nutmegged him and ran
into the penalty area.

'It's working!' Betinho shouted on the touchline.

As the goalkeeper slid out to block his shot,
Neymar Jr faked to go right as he normally did, but
then kicked the ball into the bottom corner with his
left foot.

*Goooooooooooooooooooooooooaaaaaaaaaaaaaaaalllllllll
llllllllllllllllllllll!!!!!!!!!!!!!!!!*

Neymar Jr's teammates had stopped to watch the wondergoal. They couldn't believe their eyes. Once the ball was in the net, they chased after him and jumped on top of him.

'I've never seen anything like it!'

'Those defenders are still looking for the ball now. That's magic!'

In his slightly deeper position, Neymar Jr was happy again. Even when there were four opponents surrounding him, he used the tricks and flicks that he had learnt in *futsal* and street football to escape and move his team forward. He loved the ball and he did everything he could to protect it.

'As long as you look after it too, I'll pass it to you!' Neymar Jr joked with his teammates, as they celebrated another goal. He had set it up with a killer through-ball and the smile was back on his face.

After the game, Neymar Jr hugged his coach. 'Thanks!' was all he said.

Lima was very pleased. With one small tactical switch, he had brought Neymar Jr back to life. Now there was no stopping him.

CHAPTER 9

THE BOY WHO TURNED DOWN REAL MADRID

'I know I should have told you earlier but I wanted to be 100 per cent certain before I mentioned it,' Wagner Ribeiro began. The agent looked nervous but slowly, a smile spread across his face. 'Real Madrid are interested in signing Junior!'

Neymar Sr was amazed; his son was still only thirteen years old and Real Madrid were one of the biggest clubs in the world. The boy's hero, Ronaldo, was playing there and so was Robinho, Betinho's other great discovery. Could Neymar Jr really be the latest member of their big Brazilian gang? The family truly believed in his footballing gift but this was beyond their wildest dreams.

'It's not a joke, I promise!' Wagner said when he saw Neymar Sr's shock. 'I sent them Junior's details and some videos of him in action, and they love him! They're willing to offer the kind of deal that Barcelona offered to Lionel Messi.'

If he accepted, Neymar Jr would move to Spain and begin training at the famous Madrid academy. He would learn from the best players in the world and he would earn lots of money for his family. It was an incredible deal but it had to be Neymar Jr's decision.

'Wow, that's amazing!' he shouted when he heard the news. He couldn't wait to tell all his friends at Santos. 'Where's the contract? I'll sign it right now!'

Neymar Sr laughed. 'Okay, calm down a minute! They want us to go to Madrid for a few weeks so that you can see if you like it. If you're happy, you can sign after that.'

Neymar Jr had never travelled on a plane before and neither had his dad. The trip was a big adventure for both of them. They didn't speak much Spanish and the big, busy European city was very different from the São Paulo that they were used to.

'Where's the nearest beach?' Neymar Jr asked. 'I can't imagine living this far away from the sea!'

At first, he seemed excited by all of the new experiences but after a couple of days he grew quiet. His dad noticed that something was up.

'Are you okay, son?' he asked.

Neymar Jr nodded but he didn't smile. 'It's just such a massive change for me. I'm so glad you're here, Dad; otherwise, I would probably have run away by now!'

'Junior, there's no pressure on you to stay here,' Neymar Sr said. 'I just want you to be happy playing football.'

Life was always good on the football pitch. Neymar Jr loved the modern training facilities at *La Fábrica* and he enjoyed the sessions. He was able to show off his amazing technique and he scored lots of great goals. The Real Madrid youth coaches were very impressed and the big contract was ready for Neymar Jr to sign.

But *off* the football pitch, he was finding life difficult. Everything was so scary and overwhelming.

He had met his Brazilian heroes, Ronaldo and Robinho, and watched a match in a VIP box at the huge Bernabéu Stadium. But where was the time and space to relax and have a laugh? And where were his old mates to play football with in the streets?

'Junior, you don't look happy,' his dad told him one evening as they watched a game on TV. 'You're only thirteen and there will be plenty more opportunities to come and play in Europe when you're older. The Madrid academy is excellent but if you don't feel comfortable here, you won't be able to play your best football.'

Neymar Jr felt very relieved to hear that. He had been worried about letting his dad down. 'We haven't even been here for a week yet and I already feel really homesick. I miss Mum and Rafaela, I miss my friends and I miss Santos.'

They went home to Brazil the next day. As the plane flew higher and higher above Spain, Neymar Sr looked at his son and said, 'I'm proud of you, Junior. And I'm sure you'll be back here one day.'

Neymar Jr smiled. It was really nice to know that

great clubs wanted to sign him but he wasn't quite ready to leave the familiar sights and sounds behind.

'Look, there's the beach,' he said, pointing out of the window as the plane prepared to land at São Paulo airport. 'It feels like we've been away for months!'

Once they were home, Neymar Sr phoned Wagner. 'I'm sorry but Junior wants to stay at Santos. Can you please speak to the club and ask for a better deal?'

The agent was disappointed but he spoke to the Santos President, Marcelo Teixeira.

'As you know, everyone loves Junior at this club,' Teixeira told him. 'If I said no, Zito would never leave me alone! He's the future of this club and so we'll make you a good offer.'

Some people thought Neymar Jr was crazy for rejecting such a brilliant offer from a top European team. But other people were very happy to see him again.

'He's back!' his Santos teammates cheered when he arrived at training. 'The boy who turned down Real Madrid!'

CHAPTER 10

WELCOME TO THE FIRST TEAM

'He's not even seventeen yet!' Márcio Fernándes, the Santos first team coach, argued.

'I know but did you see his goals for the Under-20s last week?' another coach asked. 'That free-kick was amazing! I think he's ready to be in the squad.'

Fernándes shook his head. 'No, I don't want to rush him. He's training with us and that's a great learning experience for him. Hopefully next year he'll be strong enough to play in the Brazilian league but right now, he's too skinny. If he tries his tricks, what do you think defenders will do? He'll be in hospital in seconds!'

Everyone at Santos was talking about Neymar Jr.

There was no doubt that he was the future of the club but the big question was: when would he make his debut?

'Junior will play soon,' was all Fernándes would say to the media.

In the end, the fans ran out of patience and the coach was sacked. The new coach, Vágner Mancini, did not wait long to select the local wonderkid.

'I'm on the bench for the home game against Oeste!' Neymar Jr told his dad. It felt so good to finally see his name on the teamsheet.

'Congratulations, I'm so proud of you!' Neymar Sr replied. He had never quite achieved his dream of playing first-team football for Santos but his son was about to do it for him. It would be the happiest day of both of their lives.

And the most nerve-wracking. The other players tried to calm him down but Neymar Jr couldn't sit still in the dressing room, or on the substitutes' bench. He was just so excited about making his Santos debut. Would he come on for five minutes? Ten minutes?

As soon as the match kicked off, the supporters were cheering for him.

Neymar! Neymar! Neymar!

'I haven't even played a match yet, and they already know my name!' he thought to himself. The Santos fans had great expectations for 'the new Pelé'. He just hoped that he could live up to that name.

Early in the second half, the score was still 0–0 and so Mancini told Neymar Jr to start warming up. As he ran along the touchline, the crowd roared and his heart began to beat even faster. He couldn't wait to entertain them with his skills.

'Be fearless out there,' Mancini told him. 'Work hard and enjoy yourself – are you ready for this?'

Neymar Jr nodded. 'I've never been so ready for anything in my life!'

He ran onto the field wearing the black-and-white shirt with the Number 18 on his back. Every Santos supporter stood up and clapped for their new hero. It was a moment that Neymar Jr would never forget. As a seven-year-old boy playing in the streets, he had often imagined playing for his local team. But the reality was much, much better than that.

The first thing he did on the pitch was untuck his shirt; he needed to play with freedom. The next thing he did was attack. As Neymar Jr dribbled towards the defender, he moved his body to go left but then moved to the right instead. It was one of his classic tricks and the defender could only stand and watch him skip away.

Neymar! Neymar! Neymar!

Out on the right wing, Neymar Jr looked up for someone to cross to in the penalty area. He aimed for the back post but he hit the ball so hard that it smacked against the bar.

'Unlucky, that would have been an amazing start!' his teammate Paulo Henrique Ganso laughed.

Whenever the Oeste defenders got the ball, Neymar Jr sprinted over to try to win it back. He had forty minutes to impress Mancini and he wasn't going to waste any of them. Each time he got the ball, he used his quick feet and speed to play one-twos and create chances for his teammates. He never stopped moving, just like his dad had taught him on the beach many years before.

'Wow, can you play like that for the whole ninety minutes?' Ganso asked him at the final whistle. Santos had won 2–1 thanks to Neymar Jr's energy and flair.

'Of course!' he replied.

'But can you play like that for the whole ninety minutes *every week?*' Ganso asked.

Neymar Jr gave a cheeky smile. 'There's only one way to find out!'

Eight days later, he was in the starting line-up for the match against Mogi Mirim.

'If you play like you did last week, you'll be fine,' Mancini said, giving him the Number 7 shirt. 'Just don't tire yourself out in the first thirty minutes!'

The big, strong defenders kicked and fouled him all game long but nothing could stop Neymar Jr from dribbling, passing and shooting. He was enjoying himself and he was desperate to get his first Santos goal.

'Relax – you'll score soon!' Mancini told him at half-time.

In the second half, Triguinho crossed the ball into the box. Neymar Jr made sure that he was onside and then threw himself forward for the diving header.

Goooooooooooooaaaaaaaaaaaaaaaaaaaallllllllllllllll lllllllll!!!!!!!!!!!!

Neymar Jr leapt into the air and punched his fist. He was so happy to score his first goal for the club. Then he pointed up at the sky to one of his biggest fans. Ilzemar had sadly died just before he could see his grandson in action for Santos, his favourite team since the days of Pelé. Neymar Jr hoped that his grandad was watching proudly from above.

As his teammates came to celebrate, Neymar Jr pointed to Triguinho and jumped into his arms. 'Thanks for the pass!' he shouted in his ear.

'No problem, welcome to the first team!' Triguinho replied.

CHAPTER 11

THE FUTURE OF BRAZIL

'Junior, wake up! Wake up!' André shouted.

'Why?' Neymar Jr mumbled. His teammate had interrupted an awesome dream about winning the World Cup for Brazil. He wasn't ready to get up yet.

'The King is here!'

Neymar Jr jumped out of bed in a flash, got dressed and ran down the corridor. At Santos, Pelé was known as 'The King'. He had scored an incredible 619 goals for the club and he still came to watch a lot of the matches. All of the Santos players were desperate to impress Pelé because the whole football world listened to him. Praise from 'The King' was a really big deal.

Neymar Jr was out of breath by the time he joined his teammates. Pelé was walking around, shaking their hands and chatting to each of them. He seemed very friendly but Neymar Jr was very nervous at meeting his hero. After all, the Santos fans were calling him 'the new Pelé'.

'The future of Brazil, it's nice to meet you!' Pelé said with a big smile on his face.

Neymar Jr smiled back but he didn't know what to say. 'The King' had just called him 'the future of Brazil'! He couldn't wait to tell his dad. 'Thanks, it's a real honour to meet you, Sir,' he managed eventually.

'I watched your debut last month – you've got skills, kid!' Pelé laughed.

Neymar Jr thanked him again. He had a question that he really wanted to ask his hero and, taking a deep breath, he plucked up the courage. 'D-do you have any advice for me, Sir?' he stuttered.

Pelé took a minute to think about his answer. 'Here in Brazil, we put so much pressure on our great footballers. They often have more responsibility than our president! My advice would be to ignore that pressure as much as you can, especially when you're so young. Enjoy your football and entertain the fans – that's all. The World Cups can wait for now!'

Neymar Jr was very grateful for Pelé's words of wisdom but 'The King' was wrong about one thing; the World Cups couldn't wait. Neymar Jr was selected in Brazil's squad for the 2009 Under-17 World Cup in Nigeria.

'It's so exciting that we get to go to Africa!' he told his teammates at the pre-tournament training camp. He already knew a few of the players from Santos but he had also made lots of new friends.

'Yes, but we're not going for a safari holiday, Junior!' joked Philippe Coutinho, a skilful midfielder who played for Vasco da Gama in Rio de Janeiro. 'We're going to Africa to win!'

Neymar Jr was full of confidence after his great start at Santos. The tournament was the perfect place to introduce himself to the world as 'the new Pelé'.

In the first match, Brazil were drawing 1–1 with Japan when Neymar Jr chased after a great pass from midfield. He was too quick for the defenders and soon he had just the goalkeeper to beat.

'Should I shoot?' Neymar Jr asked himself. No – he decided that he was too far from goal and the keeper had rushed out to block him. Instead, Neymar Jr did what street football had taught him to do: improvise. He kicked the ball around the goalkeeper and then ran through to tap it into the net.

Goooooooooooooooooooooaaaaaaaaaaaaaaaaaalllllllllllll llllllllllllllll!!!!!!!!!!!!!!!!!!!!!!!

'Great pass to yourself!' Philippe cheered as they celebrated. 'Why didn't you shoot first time?'

Neymar Jr laughed. 'Too easy!'

But after the victory against Japan, Brazil suffered a shock defeat to Mexico. Neymar Jr and Philippe were both substituted in the second half.

'That wasn't good enough,' Neymar Jr said, throwing his shinpads on the floor. He hated not playing the full ninety minutes but he accepted that he hadn't played well. 'We didn't score a single goal!'

'That Mexican defence was like a wall!' Philippe argued. 'There was just no way through.'

'No, we can't make excuses for ourselves,' Neymar Jr replied. 'With our talent, we should have found a way.'

Unfortunately, the same thing happened again in their next match, and so they were knocked out in the first round.

'I can't believe it!' Neymar Jr said on the flight back to Brazil. He was very disappointed to be leaving Nigeria so early. 'It's really embarrassing to fail like that. We were supposed to return home as heroes. That was our chance to shine!'

Philippe nodded glumly. 'Let's just hope we get another chance to make our country proud.'

The Under-17 World Cup was an important learning experience for Neymar Jr. It helped him to keep his feet on the ground as his career took off.

CHAPTER 12

FAME AND GLORY

'Junior, what have you done?!' Neymar Sr cried out. 'I told you that your hair was too long, but I didn't want you to do *that!*'

His son had just come home with a bold new 'Mohawk' haircut. The sides of his head were shaved but in the centre, there was still a strip of long hair.

'Don't you like it?' Neymar Jr asked with a smile on his face. He didn't expect his dad to like it. He liked it and his fans, the '*Neymarzetes*', would love it — that's what mattered.

In only six months, Neymar Jr's life had completely changed. He wasn't just a footballer anymore; he was a famous celebrity across the whole of Brazil. He travelled to events in Rio de Janeiro in helicopters. And every time he left his house, his fans were waiting for him. They queued for hours just to see his face and get his autograph or a photo with him. It was crazy to know that his new hairstyle would be copied by kids all over the country.

'You look like a punk,' his dad began, but he knew that it wasn't worth arguing with his son. 'Fine. As long as you play well on the pitch, I don't care about your fashion sense!'

Luckily, Neymar Jr was playing very well indeed. He had formed a great attacking trio with Ganso and André, and it got even better when Robinho made his big return to Santos.

'He's one of my heroes!' Neymar Jr told his dad happily. 'I used to watch him on TV and then pretend to be him when I played street football. Now, I'll be playing alongside him!'

Neymar Jr and Robinho became great friends straight away and together they made up cool celebrations for all the goals that the team scored.

'Remember, we're entertainers!' his hero told him.

'Now we'll be even more determined to score.'

When Neymar Jr scored from Robinho's pass against Naviraiense, his teammates rocked him like a baby and then Robinho pretended to polish his boot. And when Robinho scored from Neymar Jr's pass, the players joined hands and danced around in a circle.

'This is so much fun!' Neymar Jr shouted, with a big grin on his face. As he looked up at the crowd, the Santos fans were enjoying it just as much as the players.

In the second half, he dribbled into the penalty area with opponents all around him. He was feeling very confident. He brushed off the first defender, danced past the second, fooled the third with some fancy footwork and then dummied the goalkeeper too.

Goooooooooooooooooooooaaaaaaaaaaaaaaaaaalllllllll lllllllllllllllll!!!!!!!!!!!!!!!

'I'm sorry, I've run out of celebrations!' Robinho joked as he hugged Neymar Jr. 'That deserved something very special – it was one of the best goals I've ever seen!'

The final score against Naviraiense was 10–0 to Santos. By April 2010, the victorious team were heading towards a league and cup double: the *Campeonato Paulista* and the Copa do Brasil – the Brazilian Cup.

'If we win both, we'll be the most successful Santos team since Pelé's side in the 1960s!' Neymar Jr told Ganso. It would be amazing to go down in club history.

Against Guarani in the Copa do Brasil, Neymar Jr scored a penalty after only two minutes. He ran to one of the stewards behind the goal and collected five baseball caps. Putting them on, they danced around and pretended to be rappers. Then they threw the caps up into the crowd.

'Don't worry, I've got twenty celebrations planned for this match!' Robinho told him with a big smile.

The goals kept coming. Neymar Jr scored, then Robinho scored, then Neymar Jr scored, then Robinho scored. There was a carnival atmosphere in the Vila Belmiro Stadium but they wanted the fans to make even more noise.

'Come on!' the Santos superstars shouted, raising their arms up into the air.

The match finished 8–1, with Neymar Jr scoring five goals. He was having the time of his life.

'The newspapers are calling us "The Santastic Four" – that's brilliant!' he told his dad at dinner one night.

Neymar Sr laughed. 'It's great to see you playing with such joy, but stay focused and win these trophies. Otherwise, all those goal celebrations will look pretty silly!'

Neymar Jr nodded. He loved to have fun but he also knew when it was time to get serious.

In the semi-finals of the *Campeonato Paulista*, Santos faced their local rivals, São Paulo. They had to win the big derby but at half-time it was still 0–0.

'I missed so many great chances,' Neymar Jr said as he replayed the first half in his head. He was very frustrated with himself.

'Don't worry – we'll score,' Robinho told him. He always stayed positive.

Neymar Jr wasn't giving up. He made another run towards the six-yard box to get on the end of a cross. A defender tripped him but as he fell, he headed the ball into the net.

Gooooooooooooooooooaaaaaaaaaaaaaaaaaaaalllllllll llllllllllllllllllll!!!!!!!!!!!!!!!

Neymar Jr lifted the Santos badge on his shirt towards his lips and kissed it. He loved his home club very much and he was delighted to be their hero.

Robinho was waiting for him with a big grin on his face. 'You're always improvising, aren't you?' he said. Together, they performed the samba dance that they had practised in training.

In the final, they were up against Santo André. Santos won the away leg 3–2 but Neymar Jr knew that the tie wasn't over yet.

'We can't take it easy today,' he said in the dressing room before the home leg. 'Let's play our normal game, like the score is still 0–0.'

But his teammates didn't listen and Santos were losing 1–0 after only thirty seconds.

'Focus!' Neymar Jr shouted as the match kicked off again. They couldn't let their fans down.

Robinho flicked the ball to Neymar Jr and he dribbled into the penalty area. He glided past a few sliding tackles and curled the ball calmly into the net. One-all! Later in the match, he saved Santos again. Robinho passed to Ganso, who flicked it straight to Neymar Jr. With his weaker left foot, he slotted the ball into the bottom corner, just like his old coach Lima had taught him. Two-all!

Goooooooooooooooaaaaaaaaaaaaaallllllllllllllllllllllllll llll!!!!!!!!!!!!!!!!!!

Neymar Jr pointed at the name on the back of his shirt but it wasn't really necessary. Everyone in Brazil already knew it. He had the fame but he wanted the glory too.

The match finished 3–2 to Santo André, making it 5–5 on aggregate. But Santos were the league champions because of the number of goals they had scored earlier in the competition.

'See, I told you those goal celebrations were important!' Robinho joked.

As Neymar Jr collected his winner's medal, there were tears in his eyes. It was a very emotional day for the eighteen-year-old, especially with his family and Betinho watching proudly in the crowd. It was a great feeling to know that all of the hard work had been worth it. But the season wasn't over yet.

'Now for the double!' Neymar Jr told his teammates once the first party had ended.

In the Copa do Brasil Santos beat Vitória 3–2 on aggregate. Neymar Jr was very relieved when the referee blew the final whistle. He had missed a penalty in the first leg but thankfully, it didn't matter.

'We did it!' Robinho cheered, lifting Neymar Jr high into the air.

With forty-two goals and lots of assists, he had been the star player in a historic season for Santos. But what next for Neymar Jr? Should he stay in Brazil or move to Europe? Was he ready for a bigger challenge?

Many clubs tried to sign him but Santos didn't want to sell. In England, West Ham's £15 million offer was rejected. They wanted a lot more money than that for the best young footballer in the world – £35 million. Meanwhile, Chelsea's starting offer of £20 million was also turned down – but when they returned with a £30-million bid, the Brazilian club couldn't say no.

'It's a great deal but it's still your decision,' Neymar Sr told his son. 'Let's see what Santos say first.'

To persuade them, the club chairman made a powerful presentation, called 'Project Neymar'. 'If you stay here, we'll make sure that you become Brazil's next national sporting hero.'

That was Neymar Jr's dream and they were offering him a big new five-year contract too. Other than his hero, Ronaldo, he would be the highest paid player in the country. The phone rang and the chairman passed it to Neymar Jr. The caller was Brazil's greatest sporting hero of all: 'The King'.

'You're still very young and you still have so much more to win at Santos,' Pelé told him. 'There's no need to rush to Europe – I didn't! Wouldn't you like to win the *Copa Sudamericana*, the *Copa Libertadores* and the FIFA Club World Cup before you leave?'

For the second time in his life, Neymar Jr chose to say no to Europe, and yes to Brazil.

'I don't want to leave until I've won everything I can here,' he told his dad. 'This country needs a new national hero and that's going to be me!'

CHAPTER 13

UPS AND DOWNS

As the 2010 league season ended, the Brazilian people looked ahead to the World Cup in South Africa. After losing in the quarter-finals in 2006, they wanted the national team to do better this time and Neymar Jr was the number one hot topic.

'He hasn't even made his international debut yet!'

'Yes, but no-one else has as much creative flair as him. He could be our secret weapon!'

'He only made his league debut a year ago. We need experience in our team.'

'Don't forget that Pelé was only seventeen when we won it in 1958!'

'The King' was one of the many Brazilian legends

who argued that Neymar Jr was worth the risk but in the end, the team manager, Dunga, decided that he wasn't quite ready.

'He's a great talent for the future,' Dunga told the media, 'but right now, I want strong players who have played more football.'

Neymar Jr was disappointed to miss out but he knew that he would have many more opportunities ahead of him. He was the future of Brazil, after all.

'It's okay – this time, it's not my turn,' he told his dad. '2014 will be my turn!'

Neymar Jr watched on TV as Brazil were knocked out by the Netherlands in the quarter-finals. The whole country was very upset and the fans called for big changes.

'Why aren't the youngsters playing?' they asked angrily. 'We need to go back to the old days of exciting, Brazilian football!'

Dunga was sacked after the tournament, and the new manager, Mano Menezes, called Neymar Jr up to the squad straight away for a friendly against the USA.

'Guess what – this time I'm coming with you!' he

told Robinho, who had been playing for Brazil for years.

'And me!' Ganso added.

'And me too!' André said.

Three of 'The Santastic Four' started the match and André came on in the second half. It was a day that Neymar Jr would never forget. As he waited for kick-off, he looked down at the famous yellow Brazil shirt that he was wearing and thought back to the days when he used to play FIFA with Luiz, Dudu and Michael. They had dreamed of playing for their country and now Neymar Jr was about to make that dream come true.

'I hope they're watching!' he thought to himself.

He was determined to make a big impact. He worked hard to find space and create goalscoring chances for him and his teammates. When Robinho passed to André Santos, the left-back looked up for the cross. The ball flew over Pato's head but Neymar Jr was there at the back post. Heading wasn't his best talent but one he had worked hard to improve. He guided the ball perfectly into the bottom corner.

Goooooooooooooooooooooaaaaaaaaaaaaaaaaaaaallll llllllllllllllllllll!!!!!!!!!!!!

Neymar Jr fell to his knees and pointed to the sky. He had scored on his Brazil debut – it didn't get any better than that.

'I hope you enjoyed that, grandad!' he said to himself.

As Neymar Jr kissed the Brazil badge on his shirt, the other players celebrated with him. Robinho was right in the middle of the big team hug.

'Welcome to the team, Junior!' he shouted. 'I wish you were there at the World Cup. We needed you!'

Neymar Jr was already on the path to greatness. But at the age of still only eighteen, he still had important lessons to learn. He was playing with so much confidence that he believed he could do anything. Sometimes, however, he made mistakes.

When Neymar Jr stepped up to take the penalty in the Copa do Brasil final against Vitória, he decided to go for a Panenka, a chip down the middle of the goal. It was a brave choice because if the goalkeeper didn't dive, he would save it easily and Neymar Jr would look like a fool. And that's exactly what happened.

'What an awful penalty!' Neymar Jr said to himself, putting his hand to his face.

He tried to move on and make up for his error but the supporters in the stadium wouldn't let him forget.

Booooooooooooooooooooooooooooo!

Even the Santos fans were angry with him. 'That kid thinks he's already the best player in the world. He's too cocky!'

Neymar Jr loved to do tricks in games but sometimes they got him into trouble. Opponents didn't like his showboating at all.

'We're losing badly and he's trying to do keepy-uppies and rainbow kicks over our heads!' they complained. 'He doesn't need to show off like that. He needs to grow up and be more respectful.'

Teams also accused Neymar Jr of diving to win free-kicks and penalties. 'I know he's skinny but he goes down far too easily,' they argued. 'He's like a gymnast, jumping up into the air and then rolling around on the floor. He's cheating!'

It was a difficult time for Neymar Jr. After so many years of love and praise, the criticism really hurt him.

'I'm just trying to enjoy my football and win games for Santos,' he told his dad. 'What's wrong with that?'

'People will always be jealous of your talent,' Neymar Sr told him. 'But you have to make sure that you stay humble and kind.'

Against Atlético Goianiense, Neymar Jr dribbled into the penalty area and as he dragged the ball back, the defender fouled him. Penalty! He got up, collected the ball and walked towards the spot but his teammate Marcel stopped him.

'Sorry Junior, Coach says that I'm the penalty taker today,' he said.

Neymar Jr was furious. 'I won the penalty and I always take the penalties!' he argued.

'Calm down, mate!' Marcel replied. 'I'm only telling you what Coach told me.'

'Whatever,' Neymar Jr muttered and he threw the ball down and stormed off.

His teammates tried to talk to him but he pushed

them away; Coach Dorival shouted to him but he ignored his instructions. Neymar Jr carried on playing but he wouldn't pass to anyone.

'Who does he think he is?' the Santos fans demanded. 'No player is bigger than the team. He's become so arrogant!'

Neymar Jr just dribbled and dribbled until a defender tackled him. When the other players moaned, he shouted at them. At the final whistle, he walked straight off the pitch and went home.

After giving him an hour to think about his behaviour, his mum went to speak to him. Neymar Jr's eyes were red from crying.

'Son, what happened to you today?' Nadine asked. 'I've never seen you like that before. That's not the Junior I know – you looked like a spoilt teenager!'

'I'm sorry,' he replied. 'I just got so frustrated. I know it was really bad but it won't happen again, I promise.'

'It's not me that you need to say sorry to,' she told him. 'It's your teammates, your coaches and your fans.'

Neymar Jr nodded. It was time to grow up and take responsibility. He needed to show them that he was still the same happy, friendly, football-loving team player that he had always been. He couldn't let his success and fame go to his head.

The next morning, he spoke to the media. 'I want to apologise to everyone for what I did yesterday. It was unacceptable to act like that. I've let myself down but please forgive me for my mistakes. I'm going to improve my attitude and become a Santos hero again.'

CHAPTER 14

FOLLOWING IN THE FOOTSTEPS OF 'THE KING'

Once again, Santos were in the final of the *Campeonato Paulista*, and this time their opponents were Corinthians. After a 0–0 draw in the away leg, Neymar Jr couldn't wait to help his team to victory back home at Vila Belmiro.

'They're a good team but we've got nothing to fear!' he told Ganso.

They were now the 'Santastic Two' because Robinho and André had both left the club. Neymar Jr had even more pressure on his young shoulders but that only seemed to improve his game.

With ten minutes to go, Santos were winning 1–0. As he got the ball on the left wing, Neymar Jr had two options in his head: 1) dribble towards the corner to waste time or 2) dribble towards goal to score a second and secure the victory. He chose the second option, of course.

As the defenders backed away, Neymar Jr aimed for the bottom corner. The shot wasn't very powerful but it was very accurate.

Goooooooooooooooooooaaaaaaaaaaaaaaaaaaaaallllllll lllllllllllllllllllll!!!!!!!!!!!!!

By the time the ball trickled over the goal-line, Neymar Jr had already taken his shirt off. He had scored yet another important goal for his club. After a year of ups and downs, it was amazing to hear the fans cheering his name again at the top of their voices.

Neymar! Neymar! Neymar!

What a feeling! At the final whistle, Neymar Jr took his shirt off again. He hugged his coaches and his teammates. Together, they had won the league for the second year in a row. As Santos lifted the trophy, black and white confetti filled the air.

'We're the champions of São Paulo!' Ganso cheered.

But Neymar Jr had bigger targets in mind. 'Yes but next month, we could be the champions of the whole of South America!'

Santos had reached the quarter-finals of the *Copa Libertadores.* They hadn't won the big tournament since the 1960s, when Pelé was at his best. This was why Neymar Jr had stayed at the club – to bring the glory days back to Santos.

There was no stopping Neymar Jr. He scored a wondergoal against the Colombian team Once Caldas, and then another against Cerro Porteño from Paraguay. Santos were now only one win away from the trophy – they just had to beat Peñarol from Uruguay.

'That's the same team that Pelé beat in the final forty-eight years ago,' Neymar Sr told his son.

'Did you watch that game?' Neymar Jr asked with a big smile on his face.

'Don't be so cheeky – I wasn't even born!'

After a 0–0 draw in Uruguay, Neymar Jr felt confident that his team could win with the crowd's support back in Brazil. The match was moved to the Pacaembu Stadium so that more Santos fans could cheer them on. The players held hands as they ran on to the field and then waved to the supporters. The atmosphere was electric.

Neymar Jr's mohawk hair was even bigger than usual. He was ready to be the star but the opposition marked him very tightly. Santos had many chances to score but at half-time, it was still 0–0.

'There's no need to panic!' Neymar Jr told his teammates. He was trying to be positive like his good friend Robinho.

At the start of the second half, Arouca dribbled forward and passed to Neymar Jr on the left side of the penalty area. He shot straight away without even controlling the ball. It was a brilliant decision because the goalkeeper didn't have enough time to dive and stop it.

Goooooooooooooooooooaaaaaaaaaaaaaaaaaaaallllllll llllllllllllll!!!!!!!!!!!!!!!

Neymar Jr jumped up and punched the air. Thanks to him, Santos were now a goal ahead of Peñarol and just forty-five minutes away from winning another major trophy.

'Focus – no mistakes now!' their captain Edu Dracena shouted.

It was a tense finish but the Brazilians held on to win 2–1. The fans went wild and some even ran on to the pitch. Neymar Jr fell to the floor and pointed up to the sky. He tried to hold back his tears but he couldn't. It was the biggest moment of his life.

His family were watching in the crowd and so was Pelé. 'The King' came down on to the pitch afterwards to congratulate the players. A journalist asked him about Neymar Jr.

'He's a great player with a huge talent,' Pelé replied.

His words were ones that Neymar Jr would treasure all his life. After the trophy presentation, the celebrations moved to the dressing room. Everyone was singing and dancing and pouring champagne around. Neymar Jr loved every minute of it.

Campeones, Campeones, Olé Olé Olé.

Eventually, his dad found him at the centre of the crowd.

'Congratulations, son!' Neymar Sr said, giving him a big, emotional hug. 'I'm so proud of you.'

'Thanks!'

'You missed a couple of good chances in that second half, though,' his dad continued. 'You'll need to do some more shooting practice with your left foot.'

Neymar Jr laughed. 'Can't we talk about that tomorrow? Dad, we're the Champions of South America!'

CHAPTER 15

MEETING MESSI

'You know what this means, don't you?' Neymar
Jr said to Ganso once the celebrations were over.
'We're going to the Club World Cup in December!'

At the FIFA Club World Cup, one team
represented each football region. In 2011, it would
be Al-Sadd for Asia, Espérance for Africa, Auckland
City for Oceania, Monterrey for Central America,
Santos for South America and Barcelona for Europe.
Kashiwa Reysol from Japan were the hosts and the
sixth and last team in the tournament.

'So we might get to play against Lionel Messi?'
Ganso asked excitedly on seeing that Barcelona were
participating.

Neymar Jr nodded. 'Yes, but we'll have to get to the final first!'

In the semi-final, Santos were up against Kashiwa Reysol. Neymar Jr dyed the top of his mohawk blonde for the big day. He was ready to shine. After four minutes, his powerful shot hit the post and bounced into the goalkeeper's arms.

'Next time!' Neymar Jr said to himself. His game was brimming with confidence.

When Ganso passed to him just outside the penalty area, Neymar Jr could see a defender rushing in for the tackle. It was time to improvise. He pretended to shoot and as the defender dived in, he shifted the ball on to his left foot instead and curled a shot into the top corner. The goalkeeper didn't even have time to move.

Goooooooooooooaaaaaaaaaaaallllllllllllllllllll!!!!!!!!!!!!!!!

Neymar Jr was delighted with his start to the tournament.

'I'm not sure even Messi could have done that!' Ganso cheered.

The match finished 3–1 and Santos were through to the final against Barcelona.

'I'm confused; are you just playing one-versus-one?' Edu Dracena joked in training. 'I thought the rest of us were playing too!'

The media were nicknaming the match 'Neymar versus Messi'. Neymar Jr knew it would be a team battle but it was also an international one: Brazil versus Argentina. In addition, he was really looking forward to testing himself against Messi. The best player in the world would face the future best player in the world. Who would be victorious?

'This is my big chance to prove myself,' Neymar Jr said to his dad. He felt far more nervous than he usually did before a match.

'It's an important game because it's a final but you don't need to put any extra pressure on yourself,' Neymar Sr reassured him. 'Junior, the biggest clubs in Europe are already desperate to sign you!'

In the summer, Neymar Jr had signed a new contract at Santos, despite interest from Real Madrid, Chelsea and Manchester City. He was the Brazilian League's Player of the Year but there were still things that he wanted to achieve before he moved away.

The first was winning the FIFA Club World Cup.

Unfortunately, in the final, Santos lost 4–0 to Barcelona. Messi, Xavi and Andrés Iniesta were simply too good for Neymar Jr and co. Their pass-and-move football was so fast and skilful that the Santos players could only chase and watch as the goals went in.

'How do we even get the ball off them?!' Edu Dracena complained at half-time. 'Those guys are incredible!'

Neymar Jr tried to create something special for his team but in the end it was Messi's night. The Argentinian wizard scored two goals and won the Player of the Tournament award.

At the final whistle, Neymar Jr wiped the sweat off his face with his shirt. He had done his best for his team but it wasn't enough. He had learnt a lot of lessons, though. He hugged each of the Barcelona players but Messi was the one that he really wanted to speak to.

'Wow, that was a football masterclass,' Neymar Jr told him. 'I felt like I was back at school today. I don't know how you guys do it!'

'Thanks, you played well too,' Messi replied as

they swapped shirts. 'So when are you moving to Europe? You should come and play with me at Barcelona – it would be fun!' Neymar Jr's frown turned into a smile. 'That would be amazing!'

He always hated losing but luckily there wasn't any time for a tantrum. He had other trophies to collect. First, he travelled to Uruguay to win the South American Footballer of the Year award.

'Congratulations, you're the second Santos player to win the prize!' his dad told him.

Neymar Jr laughed. 'Let me guess who the other player was – Pelé?'

'Of course!'

Next, at the start of 2012, Neymar Jr travelled to Switzerland for the famous Ballon d'Or ceremony. He was on the shortlist for The FIFA Puskás Award for best goal of the year.

Neymar Jr's wondergoal started on the left wing, just inside the Flamengo half. With three quick flicks of his boot, he escaped from two defenders and then played a great one-two. Running at full speed towards the penalty area, he rolled the ball from his right foot to his left foot and kicked it round the last defender. It was another magical piece of skill. In the penalty area, he lifted the ball over the diving goalkeeper and into the net.

Goooooooooooooaaaaaaaaaallllllllllllllllllll!!!!!!!!!!!!!!

'And the winner of the FIFA Puskás Award is...' the presenter began, '...Neymar Jr!'

With his mohawk dyed red this time, Neymar Jr walked onto the stage. He couldn't believe what was happening. His goal had beaten brilliant strikes by Wayne Rooney and Lionel Messi.

'I'm so happy to win this award against two of my heroes,' he told the audience. 'Thank you!'

He was too nervous to say much more. He sat back down at his table and watched Messi win the Ballon d'Or for the third year in a row.

'That guy is simply amazing!' Neymar Jr said to himself. What would it be like to play with him? He was sure that Messi could teach him so much.

Later that night, the best player in the world came over to congratulate Neymar Jr. 'Remember: you, me and Barcelona. It's a match made in heaven!'

CHAPTER 16

THE HAT-TRICK

Ganso curled the free-kick into the penalty area with his brilliant left foot. His target was always the same. Neymar Jr stood between the two central defenders and waited. When the ball flew over the first defender, he was in the right place to head it powerfully past the goalkeeper.

Goooooooooooooooooaaaaaaaaaaaalllllllllllllllllllll llll!!!!!!!!!!!!!!!!!

Neymar Jr ran towards the fans and his teammates chased after him. Soon, he was in the middle of a big circle and everyone was patting him on the back and on the head. Even the substitutes joined in.

'Congratulations, Junior!' Ganso cheered. 'One hundred goals!'

Neymar Jr smiled. 'And on my twentieth birthday too – it's the best present ever!'

He was very proud of his achievement but it was still a team game, and he never forgot the defenders and midfielders who worked so hard to help him.

'I couldn't have done it without you,' Neymar Jr assured Ganso. 'We have such a great understanding – you know exactly where I'll run.'

'Yes, if you ever leave Santos, you'll have to take me with you!' Ganso joked.

Neymar Jr had prepared a special dance for the fans. He moved to the left and then moved to the right. The fans cheered loudly as the steps got faster and faster. They loved his *ginga* rhythm.

'That's enough,' the linesman told him eventually. 'We've still got thirty minutes of the match to go!'

During 2012, Neymar Jr was scoring more goals than ever. Free-kicks, penalties, headers, chips, long-range strikes, wondergoals – he scored them all.

'You're a proper striker now!' his dad told him.

'Before, every goal had to have a beautiful piece of skill but now you're happy even if you score a tap-in.'

Neymar Jr was growing up. He now had more responsibility, both on and off the pitch. After the birth of his first son, Davi Lucca, he needed to set a good example, so he saved his tricks for important moments when they could help to create goals. Otherwise, showing off didn't really help anyone. And when opponents fouled him, he tried to stay on his feet and if he couldn't, he got straight back up and carried on.

Against local rivals São Paulo in April 2012, he received the ball on the edge of the penalty area and took a shot straight away. The goalkeeper was surprised and he couldn't make a save. The strike was just too powerful.

Goooooooooooooooooooooaaaaaaaaaaaaaaaallllllllll llllllllll!!!!!!!!!!!!!!!

Santos were winning 3–1 and Neymar Jr had scored a hat-trick. He celebrated by doing his favourite thing: dancing in front of the fans.

'We're going to win three league titles in a row!' he told his dad. 'Did Pelé ever do that?'

Neymar Sr nodded. 'I'm afraid so – twice! 1960, 1961, 1962 and then 1967, 1968, 1969.'

'The King did everything – I'll never beat him.'

'No, but if you keep playing like this, you might well match him!'

There was no stopping Neymar Jr in the *Campeonato Paulista* final against Guarani. He glided past defenders as if they were just obstacles, like the mattress and the wardrobe in his childhood bedroom. He scored two goals in the first leg and Santos won 3–0. Victory was almost theirs but Neymar Jr wasn't ready to relax yet.

'I want to score another hat-trick!' he told Ganso.

When Neymar Jr had scored his first from the penalty spot after only eight minutes, the hat-trick looked likely. He took shot after shot but the goalkeeper made lots of great saves. After seventy minutes, he scored his second goal but as hard as he tried, he couldn't score a third.

'Never mind. There's always next year!' Ganso

told him at the final whistle, as the first fireworks filled the sky.

Neymar Jr wasn't too upset. How could he be when he had just got a different kind of hat-trick? Three league titles in a row! It was celebration time for Santos and Neymar Jr had planned everything carefully.

The players all wore black T-shirts saying '*Campeonato Paulista* 2010 2011 2012'. Neymar Jr also wore a white headband, just like the ones he had made for his Gremetal teammates many years before. After they lifted the trophy, there was lots of singing and dancing. By the time he got to the changing room, Neymar Jr didn't have his T-shirt or his shorts!

After a team dinner, the party really started at *Neymarzetes*, the nightclub named after his crazy fans. Neymar Jr arrived in style, driving a brand new white Porsche. He didn't leave until the early hours of the morning. He was always the life and soul of the party.

Once he had rested for a few days, Neymar Jr focused on his next goal: the 2012 London Olympics. Brazil had won silver twice and bronze twice, but never gold. It was the one trophy missing from their impressive collection. Ronaldo, Rivaldo and Ronaldinho had all tried and failed. Now it was Neymar Jr's turn.

'This is going to be our tournament!' he told Ganso confidently as they arrived in England.

There was a great team spirit in the Brazil camp and the squad was brilliant. They had the experience of Thiago Silva, Marcelo and Hulk, combined with the exciting young flair of Oscar, Pato and Neymar Jr.

The team got off to a great start with wins against Egypt, Belarus and New Zealand. Neymar Jr scored twice – his second goal was an amazing free-kick. He was playing well and the goal celebrations were excellent too.

'What are you going to do if we win gold?' Marcelo asked.

'*When* we win gold,' Neymar Jr corrected him. 'Don't worry – I've got big plans!'

He scored a penalty against Honduras in the quarter-finals and then created all three goals as Brazil beat South Korea in the semi-finals.

'Just Mexico to beat now!' Neymar Jr told Ganso.

But the Gold Medal match was a disaster for Brazil. Mexico scored in the first minute and then defended very well. Neymar Jr hardly touched the ball on the right and when he did, there was no space to work his magic.

'You need to pass it to me more quickly!' he shouted to Oscar.

Neymar Jr was becoming more and more frustrated. When he did get the chance to shoot, he kicked the ball too hard and it flew high over the bar. The match finished 2–1 to Mexico and Brazil went home with a third silver medal.

Neymar Jr sat on the pitch at Wembley, staring down at the grass. His teammates tried to help him up but he wasn't ready to move yet. He was very upset about letting his country down.

'We lost in the quarter-finals of the Copa América last year and now this,' Neymar Jr said, wiping away his tears. 'Brazil haven't won anything for years!'

'You'll have more chances to win gold,' Marcelo told him. 'The next Olympics are in Brazil and you'll need to be our star!'

CHAPTER 17

BARCELONA

In four years of first-team football, Neymar Jr had scored over 120 goals for Santos and won three league titles, one Brazilian Cup, one *Copa Libertadores* and reached the final of the Club World Cup. And he was still only twenty-one years old! By 2013, what was left for him to achieve in Brazil?

When his best friend Ganso signed for their rivals São Paulo, Neymar Jr thought long and hard about his future. Was it time to finally accept the challenge of playing in Europe? He and his dad thought so but Santos were desperate to keep him at least a little longer.

'Why don't you wait one more year?' his coach,

Muricy Ramalho, suggested. 'Stay here for the 2014 World Cup and then move to Spain.'

Brazil's legends all gave their opinion on Neymar Jr's big transfer dilemma. Pelé thought that he needed to be stronger before he played in Europe but Ronaldo thought that he was ready to test himself against the best. While everyone kept talking about him, Neymar Jr kept scoring goals but it was difficult to ignore all of the attention.

'One day, I dream of playing in Europe,' he told the Brazilian media. 'I'd like to play for a big club like Barcelona, Real Madrid or Chelsea. Who wouldn't want to play in the same team as Messi, Xavi and Iniesta? But for now, I play for Santos.'

Barcelona were very pleased to hear that they were leading the race to sign Neymar Jr. The club had been following his progress for years but it was now time to make an offer. Messi, their superstar, needed a partner in attack and the club believed that the Brazilian was the best man for the job.

However, Barcelona's big rivals Real Madrid hadn't given up on Neymar Jr, despite their disappointment

seven years earlier when he had chosen to stay in
Brazil. Barcelona were the Spanish League winners
but Real were the Champions League winners.
Cristiano Ronaldo, their superstar, also needed a
partner in attack.

'How does it feel to have the two biggest clubs in
the world fighting over you?' Neymar Sr asked his
son with a smile.

'It's tiring!' he replied. 'I need to take some time to
think about each offer and make my decision.'

In the end, Neymar Jr chose the style of Barcelona
and the chance to play with Messi. He left the
contract negotiations to his dad and his agent,
Wagner Ribeiro, and began his long goodbye to
Santos. Despite his best efforts, however, he couldn't
win a fourth *Campeonato Paulista* for his club. That
would have been the perfect leaving present.

'I am going but I'll be back!' he wrote on the wall
at the training ground.

Next, he told his *Neymarzetes* around the world.
'On Monday I will sign for Barcelona,' he posted on
Twitter, Facebook and Instagram. 'I want to thank all

the Santos fans for these ten incredible years. I will always be Santos!'

Over 60,000 fans came to watch Neymar Jr's final match for Santos in May 2013 against Flamengo. It was a very emotional day and he was crying even before the game kicked off. He was desperate to be the matchwinner yet again. Neymar Jr's free-kick flew towards the top corner but the Flamengo goalkeeper made a great save.

'The keeper should have let that in on purpose!' Neymar Sr joked to Nadine. 'Junior deserves to say goodbye in style.'

In the end, it finished 0–0. As he left the pitch for the last time, Neymar Jr clapped and waved to the fans. He would never forget their love, energy and support. When he threw his shirt into the crowd, a fight nearly broke out.

Neymar Jr arrived in Barcelona on a private jet. He posed for photos next to the club badge with his baseball cap on backwards and a big smile on his face. It was still hard to believe that his dream was really coming true. After medical tests, Neymar Jr went to the Nou Camp to sign his five-year contract.

'Are you ready for this?' Sandro Rosell, the club chairman, asked him.

Neymar Jr nodded. He knew what happened next. Once he was dressed in the Barcelona kit, he walked out onto the blue carpet that covered the pitch. The 56,000 fans in the stadium roared. They had been queueing for hours to meet their new signing.

Neymar! Neymar! Neymar!

'Welcome, Neymar Jr!' was written on the big screen.

He had played football in front of very big crowds before but this was a completely different experience. There were no teammates by his side; it was just him: The Neymar Jr Show. He turned around in circles, waving to everyone.

Luckily, he had a football in his hands. Since he was very young, Neymar Jr had always felt safer with a football. It was his safety blanket. On the stage, he did some keepy-uppies to entertain the fans.

Now, Neymar Jr had to make his speech. It was the part that he had been dreading for weeks. As a

Brazilian, he spoke Portuguese and a bit of Spanish. But the people of Barcelona had a language of their own – Catalan. He had been learning one phrase all day.

'Hello, I'm very happy to be a Barcelona player. It is a dream come true. *Visca el Barca!*'

The supporters went wild. *Neymar! Neymar! Neymar!*

Neymar Jr's last task of the day was to speak to the Spanish journalists. He had a clear message for them.

'Barca is a great team and I want to help Messi to continue to be the greatest player in the world,' he told them.

Some people were worried that the two superstars wouldn't play well together in the same team but Neymar Jr was very happy to support Messi. He knew that he still had a lot to learn, especially in European football, and the Argentinian was his friend and hero.

'What a day!' Neymar Jr said to himself as he returned to his hotel.

He was exhausted but he didn't have long to rest. In a few days, Neymar Jr would be returning home to play in the Confederations Cup.

CHAPTER 18

CONFEDERATIONS CUP

Brazil were the hosts for the 2013 FIFA Confederations Cup, a tournament featuring the best teams from around the world: Uruguay also from South America, Spain and Italy from Europe, Japan from Asia, Nigeria from Africa, Mexico from Central America, and Tahiti from Oceania.

'This is our warm-up for next year's World Cup,' Brazil's coach Luiz Felipe Scolari told his players. 'Let's show what we can do!'

Brazil had won the tournament in 2005 and 2009 but could they make it three wins in a row? Most of the players had played together at the 2012 Olympics but Neymar Jr had one new teammate in attack: Fred.

'I'm here to score goals,' Fred told Hulk, Oscar and Neymar Jr happily. 'You guys do the skills and I'll just make sure that the ball goes in the net!'

Neymar Jr now wore the famous Number 10 shirt, passed down to him by legends like Zico, Rivaldo, Ronaldinho and, of course, Pelé. It put even more pressure on his skinny shoulders but Neymar Jr didn't mind at all. With a smart new shorter haircut, he was ready to show that he could lead his country to glory.

In the first match against Japan, Fred chested the ball down and Neymar Jr hit a beautiful shot into the top corner. 1–0 – what a start!

Brazil's second match was against Mexico, a repeat of the 2012 Olympic Final. It was time for revenge. When Dani Alves put an early cross into the box, the defender headed it away but straight to Neymar Jr. He watched the ball carefully as it fell and hit a sweet volley into the bottom corner.

Goooooooooooooooooooaaaaaaaaaaaaaaaaalllllllllllllll lllllllllllll!!!!!!!!!!!!!!!!

The Brazilian supporters went wild as Neymar Jr ran towards them and jumped into the air. This time, he wouldn't let his country down.

'What a strike!' Marcelo screamed as he jumped on the hero.

In the last minute, Neymar Jr set up a second goal to complete his 'man of the match' performance.

Brazil were already through to the semi-finals but Neymar Jr didn't want to miss the final group game against Italy.

'I'm ready to play!' he told Scolari.

'I know but we need you at your very best in the next match,' his manager replied. 'And what if you get hurt in this game?'

'Please let me start,' Neymar Jr begged. 'If we're winning, you can take me off for the last twenty minutes.'

In the end, Scolari agreed. After all, he needed to keep his star player happy.

Early in the second-half, Brazil won a free-kick just outside the penalty area. It would be difficult to beat a world-class keeper like Gianluigi Buffon but

Neymar Jr was fearless. His shot flew like an arrow into the corner of the net.

Goooooooooooooooooooaaaaaaaaaaaaaaaalllllllllllll llllllll!!!!!!!!!!!!!!!!

He pointed to the number on his back – yes, he was more than good enough to wear the 10. He was a superstar. With twenty minutes left to go, Neymar Jr left the pitch to a standing ovation.

It was a South American semi-final – Brazil vs Uruguay.

'We've played so well so far,' Scolari told the team. 'We just need two more great performances – we can't lose to our local rivals!'

At the end of the first half, Neymar Jr chested the ball down as he ran into the penalty area and tried to lift it over the keeper. The keeper saved it but Fred was there to score the rebound. 1–0! Fred ran to the fans and Neymar Jr jumped up on his back.

'You're a goal-hunter, always waiting for your next chance to score!'

Uruguay equalised but Brazil never gave up. With

five minutes to go, Paulinho scored from Neymar Jr's corner to put them through to the final.

'Rio here we come!' Dani Alves shouted as the whole squad celebrated. The final would be played at the Maracanã Stadium in Rio de Janeiro, in front of more than 70,000 supporters.

'And at least 90 per cent of the crowd will be Brazilians!' Neymar Jr added. He couldn't wait for the big day.

Their opponents would be Spain, the 2010 World Cup and Euro 2012 winners. Neymar Jr and Dani Alves would be playing against their Barcelona club-mates Gerard Piqué, Sergio Busquets, Xavi and Andrés Iniesta. For one day only, they would be enemies.

'There's only one way to test how good we are,' Scolari said to his players. 'And that's by taking on the best team in the world.'

Neymar Jr had never been so excited about a match in his life. With just two minutes gone, Brazil scored after a goalmouth scramble.

'You kicked that in while lying on the floor!' Neymar Jr shouted.

Fred smiled. 'I was in the right place at the right time again!'

Just before half-time, Neymar Jr got the ball on the edge of the penalty area. He took one touch and then smashed his shot into the roof of the net with his left foot. The goalkeeper didn't have a chance.

Goooooooooooooooooooooooaaaaaaaaaaaaaaallllllllllll llllllllllllll!!!!!!!!!!!!!!!

Neymar Jr ran straight into the waiting arms of the Brazilian fans. It was the best feeling in the world to make them so happy.

'Wow, how do you kick it that hard?' Oscar asked him as they ran back for the restart. 'You're as skinny as me!'

Neymar Jr had a good answer for that. 'Hard work and a gift from God.'

In the second half, Neymar Jr dribbled forward from his own half. They were winning 3–0 but he always wanted to score more. Piqué backed away, scared of Neymar Jr's skill and speed. As the Brazilian shifted the ball to the left, Piqué went for the tackle but he was too late to win the ball. Instead, he fouled Neymar Jr and got a red card.

At the final whistle, Iniesta hugged Neymar Jr. 'What a performance! There was nothing that we could do to stop you today. Just make sure that you play like that for Barcelona this season!'

Neymar Jr didn't stop smiling for days. The 2013 Confederations Cup was a time that he would never forget. He won the award for the tournament's best player but it was a brilliant team effort. Together, the Brazilians had made their nation proud again.

'We won every match and beat the World Champions,' Neymar Jr said to Dani Alves. 'Bring on the World Cup now!'

CHAPTER 19

NEW START
IN SPAIN

In the 2013 Spanish Super Cup, league winners
Barcelona faced cup winners Atlético Madrid.
Neymar Jr was determined to get off to a great start
but Barcelona's manager Gerardo Martino chose to
play a front three of Lionel Messi, Pedro and Alexis
Sánchez.

'Don't worry – you'll get your chance in the
second half,' Martino told him. He didn't want to
rush his new superstar.

Neymar Jr watched from the bench as Barcelona
went 1–0 down. He was raring to get out there and
help his team but when Lionel came off at half-time,
it was Cesc Fàbregas who replaced him.

'There's still plenty of time,' Neymar Jr told himself. He needed to be patient.

After sixty minutes, Neymar Jr finally entered the game, wearing the Number 11 shirt. As Dani Alves attacked down the right, he ran from the left wing towards the penalty area. The Brazilian teammates knew each other well. The cross was perfect and Neymar Jr headed the ball into the bottom corner.

Goooooooooooooooooooaaaaaaaaaaaaaaaaaallllllllllll llllllllllll!!!!!!!!!!!!!!!

It was an amazing feeling to score his first official goal for Barcelona. Neymar Jr ran straight to Dani Alves and jumped into his arms. Xavi, Andrés and Alexis hugged him too.

'Welcome to Barca!' they all cheered.

It was exactly what Neymar Jr needed as he adapted to his new life in Spain. He missed Brazil and his old club. At Santos, they never worried about his size. They believed that being small and skinny helped him to skip past defenders but Barcelona wanted him to build lots of muscle.

'I hate the gym!' Neymar Jr told his dad.

'I know but you have to listen to your coaches,' Neymar Sr replied. 'They want to make you an even better player.'

That was why Neymar Jr had come to Barcelona – to improve. He wasn't scoring as many goals as he had at Santos but he was playing well for the team and creating lots of chances for Lionel.

'The fans love you!' Dani Alves reassured him. 'You're doing exactly what Martino has asked you to do.'

Soon it was time for Neymar Jr's biggest test – Barcelona vs Real Madrid, his first *El Clásico*. It was the battle of the superstars: Neymar Jr and Messi against Cristiano Ronaldo and Gareth Bale. Who would win?

'Are you ready to shine?' Lionel asked him as they waited in the tunnel.

Neymar Jr could already hear the incredible noise of the Nou Camp crowd. He had never heard anything like it. There were nearly 100,000 fans in the stadium. 'You bet I am!' he replied. He was buzzing.

Neymar Jr ran past one defender and then cut inside past another. He took a shot but he fell over as he kicked it and the goalkeeper made a comfortable save. Undeterred, Neymar Jr got back up and carried on.

'Take your time,' Lionel told him.

A few minutes later, Andrés dribbled through the middle and passed to Neymar Jr on the left side of the penalty area. He took Lionel's advice and placed his shot carefully through the defender's legs and into the far corner. The goalkeeper could only turn and watch the ball go in.

Goooooooooooooooooooaaaaaaaaaaaaaaaaaaaallllllllllll lllllllllllll!!!!!!!!!!!!!

Lionel ran to celebrate with his strike partner. 'What a clever finish!' he screamed.

It was certainly one of the best moments of Neymar Jr's life. All of his teammates hugged him and the fans chanted his name.

Neymar! Neymar! Neymar!

Barcelona won 2–1 and Neymar Jr was the big game hero.

'I'm so glad we signed you!' Lionel told him as they walked around the pitch, thanking the supporters.

In December, Lionel was injured and so Neymar Jr

got his chance as Barcelona's central striker. He didn't let his team down. He scored his first Champions League hat-trick in a 6–1 victory over Celtic and then both goals in a 2–1 win over Villarreal.

'Five goals in four days – you're on fire!' Cesc shouted.

Neymar Jr was enjoying his new life in Spain enormously. But just when he was finding his best form, disaster struck. Against Getafe, he dribbled down the left wing and as he stretched to cross the ball, he twisted his right ankle.

Owwwwwwwwwwwww!

As he lay on the grass in agony, Cesc ran over. 'What happened?'

Neymar Jr was in too much pain to speak. All he could do was raise his arm in the air to ask for help. With the physios supporting his weight, he limped off. The supporters were very sad to see him go.

'How bad is it?' he asked as he sat on the treatment table. Each movement of the ankle hurt so much.

'The good news is that it's not broken,' the team

doctor told him. 'The bad news is that it's sprained. You'll need to rest it for at least a month.'

Neymar Jr was frustrated to miss so many matches but he focused on recovering as quickly as possible. His team needed him.

By the middle of February 2014, Neymar Jr was fit enough to be on the bench again. As Barcelona were beating Rayo Vallecano 4–0, Martino told him to warm up. When Neymar Jr ran on to the pitch, the fans chanted his name. It was great to be back in action and there was plenty of time to grab a goal.

Alexis passed to Andrés, who passed to Neymar Jr just inside the Rayo Vallecano half. The Brazilian had lots of space to run. He glided past one tackle and as the defenders backed away, he decided to shoot. He was at least thirty yards away from goal but Neymar Jr had nothing to lose. The ball flew into the top corner.

Goooooooooooooooaaaaaaaaaaaaaaaaaaallllllllllllllllllll llllllll!!!!!!!!!!!!!!!!!!!

What a return! Neymar Jr ran to the fans and jumped into the air. Then he looked for Dani Alves. They had prepared a special dance.

'Next time, you need to do more practice,' Neymar Jr joked with his teammate. 'Robinho is a much better dancer!'

Unfortunately, Neymar Jr's first season at Barcelona ended in disappointment. They were beaten by Atlético Madrid in the Champions League and the Spanish League, and also by Real Madrid in the Spanish Cup.

'I can't believe it – we didn't win any trophies this year!' Neymar Jr said to Lionel. Losing to their bitter rivals was hard to accept.

'I know, this can't happen again,' he replied. 'Next season, we'll have to win everything.'

Neymar Jr nodded and managed a smile. He was satisfied with his start in Spain but there was plenty of room for improvement.

'Right, we need to stop talking to each other now!' Lionel joked.

Neymar Jr laughed. 'Oh yeah! For the next six weeks, we're not friends – we're enemies!'

It was time for the massive tournament that they had both been waiting for: the 2014 World Cup.

CHAPTER 20

WORLD CUP 2014

'When I was young, I watched Romário and Ronaldo win World Cups,' Neymar Jr told the media. 'Now I want to do that too and this time, it will be right here in Brazil!'

As the first match got closer, the pressure only increased. There was no Kaká, no Pato, no Robinho and no Ronaldinho. So all hopes rested on Brazil's star Number 10, Neymar Jr. After some difficult years, the country was desperate for a reason to celebrate.

'We played so well together at the Confederations Cup last year and everyone's back here again,' Dani Alves reassured Neymar Jr. 'You won't be doing this alone!'

Neymar Jr believed in himself and his teammates but he knew that it would be very difficult to make his nation happy. Brazil were one of four favourites to win, alongside Germany, Iniesta and Xavi's Spain, and Lionel's Argentina. With his hair dyed blonde, Neymar Jr was determined to shine.

After ten minutes of Brazil's opening match against Croatia, Marcelo scored an own goal. The big crowd in the São Paulo Arena fell silent. It was the worst possible start for Brazil. They needed Neymar Jr's magic, and quickly.

When Oscar passed to him, Neymar Jr was still forty yards from goal. But the Croatian defence backed away and gave him the space to dribble forward. Suddenly, the Brazil fans were excited.

Shoot! Shoot! Shoot!

From just outside the penalty area, Neymar Jr hit the ball with his left foot through a crowd of legs. It wasn't his most powerful strike but it was deadly accurate. The goalkeeper dived across but he couldn't quite reach it as it rolled right into the corner.

Goooooooooooooooooooooaaaaaaaaaaaaaaaaaaalllllllll llllllllllllllllllll!!!!!!!!!!!!!

The sea of yellow shirts danced in the stands but down on the pitch, Neymar Jr hardly made time to celebrate. Instead, he ran straight back for the restart. He wanted to score again as soon as possible.

'Come on!' he shouted to his teammates.

With twenty minutes to go, Fred won a penalty and Neymar Jr had the chance to put Brazil ahead. He just had to stay calm. He ran up slowly and kicked it as hard as he could. The goalkeeper dived the right way but he managed to push the ball into the roof of the net.

Goooooooooooooooooooooaaaaaaaaaaaaaaaaaaalllllllllll llllllllllllllllllll!!!!!!!!!!!!!

This time, Neymar Jr did celebrate. He ran towards the fans and his teammates joined him. It hadn't been their best performance but thanks to their superstar, Brazil had won the game. That was all that really mattered.

'We need to be much better next time,' Scolari warned his players.

But against Mexico, Brazil played even worse. Neymar Jr was marked closely and without his creativity, the team struggled. It finished 0–0.

'At least we didn't lose,' Dani Alves said afterwards, trying to stay positive.

'That's true but we're here to win!' Neymar Jr replied, kicking the air in frustration. 'If we play like that again, we might not make it to the second round.'

The Brazilian people were not impressed. They demanded more from their countrymen in their final group stage game against Cameroon. Luiz Gustavo dribbled down the left wing and put a perfect cross into the box. Neymar Jr ran between the centre-backs and sidefooted the ball into the net. He made it look so easy.

Goooooooooooooooooooaaaaaaaaaaaaaaaaaaaallllllllll llllllllllllll!!!!!!!!!!!!!

'That's more like it!' he cheered.

But ten minutes later, Cameroon had equalised. Neymar Jr needed to do it all over again. As he dribbled across the penalty area, the goalkeeper dived one way and he shot the other way, through the legs of the defender.

Goooooooooooooooooaaaaaaaaaaaaaaaaaaaalllllllllll lllllllll!!!!!!!!!!!!!!!

'I thought you said I wouldn't be doing this on my own!' Neymar Jr joked as Dani Alves ran over to hug him. He was very happy to be the hero.

In the second round, Brazil faced their South American rivals Chile. It was a very tense match. David Luiz's goal calmed Brazil down but when Neymar Jr's Barcelona teammate Alexis made it 1–1, the host team became very nervous. If they made one mistake, they could be knocked out and the nation would be furious. In the end, it went to penalties.

'I'll take the last one,' Neymar Jr told Scolari. That gave him a little time to rest. He was exhausted after 120 minutes of football.

Neymar Jr stood with his teammates on the halfway line and waited. After eight penalties, it was 2–2. It was his turn. The walk to the penalty area seemed to take forever. The referee handed him the ball and Neymar Jr put it down carefully on the spot. Despite all of the noise and pressure, he felt calm. He sent the goalkeeper the wrong way and scored.

'Come on, save this last penalty and we win!' Neymar Jr shouted to Júlio César as they high-fived.

Júlio didn't have to save it; the ball hit the post. The Brazil players ran to celebrate with their keeper.

'We did it!' Neymar Jr screamed with relief. He fell to his knees on the pitch and began to cry tears of joy and relief. Their World Cup dream was still alive.

Against Colombia in the quarter-finals, Brazil's captain Thiago Silva scored an early goal from Neymar Jr's corner and David Luiz made it 2–0 with an incredible free-kick. It was all looking good for Brazil, even when Colombia scored a penalty.

But in the last few minutes, as Neymar Jr went to chest the ball down, his opponent pushed his knee into his back.

Owwwwwwwwwwwwwwww!

Neymar Jr fell to the floor and screamed with pain. The crowd went quiet and Marcelo rushed over to him.

'What happened? Are you okay?'

'I don't know but I can't feel my legs!'

As Neymar Jr was carried off on a stretcher, he cried and cried. He feared that his World Cup was over.

'I'm afraid you've fractured one of the vertebrae in your back,' the team doctor told him.

Neymar Jr thought he knew the awful answer but he had to ask. 'Is there any chance that I can play in the semi-final against Germany?'

The team doctor shook his head sadly. 'I'm afraid you need to rest for at least a month.'

The whole of Brazil was devastated, from the players to the fans. How could they continue without their superstar and leader?

'You can do it without me,' he told his teammates. 'I'll be cheering you on!'

For the semi-final, however, he didn't cheer them on live at the Mineirão Stadium. He needed to rest and he knew it would be a nightmare to be so close to the pitch when he couldn't help his country. Instead, he watched the game at home with his friends and family. It turned out to be the worst TV that Neymar Jr had ever seen.

'That's it – I'm turning it off!' he shouted as Germany scored yet another goal, to make it 7–0.

It was too painful to watch any more. Without Neymar Jr, Brazil completely fell apart and suffered their most humiliating defeat of all time.

'We have to move on,' he told his teammates the next day. They were all still in shock. They didn't dare look at what the newspapers were saying about them. 'The preparations for World Cup 2020 start today!'

CHAPTER 21

THE TREBLE

'Let's just forget about the World Cup and focus on the new season,' Lionel said to Neymar Jr. Lionel was upset too because his Argentina team had lost to Germany in the final.

The Brazilian smiled. 'Sounds good to me!'

As his back injury healed, Neymar Jr got ready to show the Barcelona fans just how good he could be. He now had a year's experience of Spanish football and a year's experience of playing with Lionel.

'This is going to be your season!' Dani Alves predicted.

There had been some major changes at Barcelona.

Cesc and Alexis had both moved to England, team captain Carles Puyol had retired and Martino had resigned as manager. Former player Luis Enrique was the new man in charge and Lionel and Neymar Jr had a new partner in attack: the Uruguayan striker Luis Suárez.

'Welcome to Barca!' they said to Luis on his first day in training. 'Let's score lots of goals and win lots of trophies together!'

Soon, the whole football world was talking about 'MSN' – Messi, Suárez, Neymar Jr.

Neymar Jr dribbled in from the left and passed to Luis. Luis flicked the ball through for the one-two and Lionel was already making his run to the back-post to tap in Neymar Jr's cross.

Goooooooooooooooooooaaaaaaaaaaaaaaaaaallllllllllll llllllllllll!!!!!!!!!!!!!!!

'It's like we've been playing together for years!' Lionel joked as the three superstars hugged.

'Don't forget about me!' Andrés shouted as he joined them.

And Neymar Jr wasn't just setting up goals for Luis

and Lionel; he was also scoring lots of goals of his own, like the good old days at Santos.

'I've already scored as many goals as I scored in the whole of last season and it's not even November yet!' he told Lionel.

Barcelona lost *El Clásico* against Real Madrid's 'BBC' – Gareth Bale, Karim Benzema and Cristiano Ronaldo – but they were still top of the Spanish League and had reached the knockout stages of the Champions League.

'We're still on for the Treble!' Dani Alves said confidently.

That was the team's big target. Against Paris Saint-Germain in the Champions League quarter-finals, Andrés dribbled forward and passed to Neymar Jr. He glided past his Brazilian teammate David Luiz, rounded the keeper and tapped the ball into the net.

Gooooooooooooooooooooaaaaaaaaaaaaaaaalllllllllllllllll llllllllllll!!!!!!!!!!!!!!!!!

'Great pass!' Neymar Jr shouted as he hugged Andrés.

'Great finish!' his teammate replied.

Twenty minutes later, Neymar Jr scored again to send Barcelona through to a semi-final against Bayern Munich. Everyone was excited about the battle of the two best teams in the world. Bayern's manager was Pep Guardiola, the man who had won everything with Barcelona a few years earlier.

'Pep was one of the reasons that I wanted to come to Barcelona,' Neymar Jr told his teammates.

'But I was the main reason, right?' Lionel said and everyone laughed.

In the first leg at the Nou Camp, the Argentinian was the hero. He scored two goals and then played a great through-ball for Neymar Jr. In the penalty area he faked to shoot one way, faked to shoot the other way and then shot through the keeper's legs.

Goooooooooooooooooooooaaaaaaaaaaaaaaaalllllllllllll llllllllllllll!!!!!!!!!!!!!!!

Neymar Jr and Lionel rolled around on the grass together, and Luis joined them. MSN were having so much fun.

In the second leg, Neymar Jr and Luis were the joint heroes. Neymar Jr scored both goals and in each case Luis set them up. Barcelona were through to another Champions League final.

'I know you're an old pro now but Luis and I are excited!' Neymar Jr joked with Lionel. 'This is our first time in the final!'

Before that, Barcelona had two other trophies to win. Lionel's goal secured the Spanish League title and then Lionel and Neymar Jr's goals secured the Spanish Cup. The team celebrated both achievements but they knew that their biggest test was still to come.

'It's time for the Treble!' Dani Alves reminded them.

With one game left in the season, Neymar had scored thirty-eight goals and MSN had scored 120 in total.

'We're officially the best front three ever!' Luis reported.

But to really go down in history, they had to win the Champions League final against Italian giants Juventus in Berlin. Neymar Jr wasn't nervous ahead of the biggest match of his life; he was focused on winning.

In the first few minutes, he played the ball into Andrés's path as he ran into the penalty area. He passed to Ivan Rakitić, who scored. 1–0!

'When we play flowing football like that, we're unstoppable!' Neymar Jr shouted as they celebrated.

But after sixty-five minutes, Juventus had equalised. Barcelona needed more goals. MSN to the rescue! Lionel ran through the middle, dribbled past one defender and then created a powerful shot. The ball swerved through the air and the keeper could only push it away. Luis was ready for the rebound. 2–1 to Barcelona!

Neymar Jr and Lionel chased after their strike partner as he ran around the pitch. Eventually, they caught up with Luis and they celebrated in style with the fans.

'We're nearly there!' they cheered.

Barcelona kept attacking. Jordi Alba made a great run down the left and crossed into the box. Neymar Jr was there to flick the ball into the bottom corner. He began to celebrate but his smile quickly changed to a frown. The referee had disallowed the goal for handball.

'No way!' Neymar Jr said, waggling his finger from

side to side and shaking his head. 'It hit my shoulder, not my arm.'

But the referee wouldn't listen.

'Keep going!' Andrés told Neymar Jr. 'There's still time to score again.'

With seconds to go, Lionel played a brilliant through-ball to Neymar Jr. As he ran towards goal, he passed to Luis, who then passed back to him. The tired Juventus defenders couldn't cope with their brilliant teamwork. As he entered the penalty area, Neymar Jr struck the ball with his left foot and it flew through the goalkeeper's legs.

Goooooooooooooooooaaaaaaaaaaaaaaaallllllllllllllllll llllllllll!!!!!!!!!!!!!!!!!

This time, the goal counted. What a moment! Neymar Jr took his shirt off and ran towards the supporters, pumping his fists like crazy. It was the perfect way to finish an incredible year. He had scored in his first Champions League final and Barcelona had won the Treble.

'It doesn't get any better than this!' Dani Alves screamed as they hugged each other.

With a Brazil flag wrapped around his waist, Neymar Jr walked around the stadium, holding hands with Davi Lucca. Both father and young son had matching '11 Neymar Jr' shirts and matching white headbands too.

'Wave to the fans!' he said as he lifted Davi into the air like a trophy. His son was proudly wearing his winner's medal around his neck. 'They love you already.'

It was party time for Barcelona. Neymar Jr jumped up and down with his teammates. He was delighted to be one of the heroes. After a decent first season at Barcelona, he had come back so much more strongly for a super second season.

CHAPTER 22

MSN

'What do you think?' Neymar Jr asked as he arrived for a training session. His teammates were used to seeing his new hairstyles each week but this one was really radical.

Lionel and Luis look shocked. 'Where did all your hair go?'

'Dani Alves said it would look cool!' Neymar Jr said as he rubbed his shaved head.

Lionel laughed. 'You're very brave to let him touch your hair!'

'Yeah, if I wanted style advice, Dani Alves is the last person I would speak to!' Luis added.

The Nou Camp crowd was also surprised by

Neymar Jr's new look but as long as MSN kept scoring goals, they didn't mind.

Against Rayo Vallecano in October 2015, Neymar Jr dribbled forward and then slowed down to think about his options. Luis was calling for the ball in the middle but with a burst of pace, he kept dribbling. The defender couldn't keep up; all he could do was foul him. Penalty! Neymar Jr took it himself and scored.

Goooooooooooooooaaaaaaaaaaaaaaaaaalllllllllllllllll lllllllll!!!!!!!!!!!!!!!!!!!!!!

Ten minutes later, he did it again. This time, Neymar Jr's skill was even more magical. He rolled the ball from one foot to the other and did a step over and then a nutmeg, all in one movement. The defender had no idea what was going on and stuck out his leg to trip him. Penalty! Neymar Jr scored again.

'Are you ever going to pass to me?' Luis joked.

'Not when I can beat them on my own!' Neymar Jr replied with a smile. 'This new haircut has given me super powers.'

With Lionel out injured, Neymar Jr was enjoying

his starring role. Just before half-time, he raced into the box once more and a defender kicked him again. But this time, the referee waved to play on. Neymar Jr was furious.

'How was that not a foul?' he complained to Luis.

'Don't be so greedy!' his strike partner teased him. 'The referee can't give you three penalties in twenty minutes.'

Neymar Jr's glory was not over. In the second half, he scored his third and fourth goals of the match. He celebrated like the old days at Santos with Robinho. Dani Alves pretended to polish his boots and then he danced for the fans.

'What a performance!' Luis said as they high-fived after the final whistle.

'It was my turn today,' Neymar Jr told him. 'It will be your turn next week!'

He would be right. Against Eibar, Barcelona won 3–1. Luis scored a hat-trick, although even then Neymar set up two of the goals.

'I'm not sure we need our "M",' Luis laughed. 'How does "SN" sound?'

'I prefer "NS"!' Neymar Jr replied cheekily.

The 'M' would soon make a comeback of sorts; Lionel was back for the first *El Clásico* of the season but he was only on the bench. Neymar Jr and Luis would have to take on Real Madrid's 'BBC' without him.

'Don't worry – you'll be able to take it easy when you come on!' they told Lionel.

They were both playing with joy and confidence. By half-time, Barcelona were winning 2–0 and Neymar Jr and Luis had scored one goal each. By full-time, they had thrashed their rivals 4–0 away at the Bernabéu.

'What a win!' Neymar Jr shouted as his team celebrated a memorable victory.

Barcelona were top of the Spanish League and it was soon time to travel to Japan to challenge for another trophy – the 2015 FIFA Club World Cup. It was a particularly important one for Neymar Jr.

'I was so upset when I lost in the final with Santos four years ago,' he told Lionel. 'Do you remember? I was crying on the pitch!'

How times had changed. Now Neymar Jr was a Barcelona star and he was determined to collect a winner's medal. He would be absent through injury for the semi-final against China's Guangzhou Evergrande but he returned for the final against Argentina's River Plate. Although he didn't score on that occasion, both Lionel and Luis did.

'Thanks, I feel much better now!' he told his teammates as they stood with the medals around their necks.

The good times continued in 2016. Neymar Jr was back at the Ballon d'Or ceremony and this time, he was on the shortlist for the Best Player in the World award.

'Congratulations, son! You deserve this after winning the Treble last season,' his dad told him as they arrived in Switzerland together.

Neymar Jr was sure that either Cristiano or Lionel would win the top prize but it was great to be one of the other players on the list, alongside amazing players like Luis and Andrés. He didn't worry about writing a winning speech.

'I'm going to enjoy myself tonight!' Neymar Jr told his Barcelona teammates.

He was wearing a very cool suit for the big day with a velvet waistcoat, a spotted bow-tie and a bowler hat. He stopped to take lots of photos on the red carpet outside.

'My fans will love these on Instagram!' he told his dad as they took a selfie together.

When Lionel won the Ballon d'Or, he turned to Neymar Jr and they kissed each other on the cheek. The Brazilian was delighted for his Barcelona strike partner and he was delighted for himself too – he had finished third, behind Cristiano but ahead of his other teammates.

'I'll beat you next year!' Luis said, displaying his competitive spirit.

Unfortunately, Barcelona were knocked out of the Champions League in the quarter-finals, but they still finished top of the Spanish League and faced Sevilla in the final of the Spanish Cup.

'I wanted to win another treble this season but the double will have to do,' Neymar Jr told his teammates before kick-off. He was desperate to end the season in style.

'Did Dani Alves cut your hair again?' Lionel joked, pointing at Neymar Jr's new slicked-back look.

'At least I try new things – you're just boring!' he replied with a smile.

As soon as the game against Sevilla started, MSN got serious. But when their defender Javier Mascherano was sent off in the first half, Barcelona's Spanish double was in danger. Luis went off injured early in the second half but Luis Enrique kept Neymar Jr on the pitch. His manager trusted him to be the matchwinner. He worked hard in defence and attacked at every opportunity.

In injury time, Neymar Jr raced on to Lionel's through-ball but just outside the penalty area, he was fouled, to his great disappointment.

'I was going to score the winner!' he moaned as he got back to his feet.

'There's still time for that,' Andrés reminded him.

In extra-time, Lionel set up goals for Jordi Alba and then Neymar Jr. After he slid the ball past the goalkeeper, Neymar Jr ran over to hug Lionel.

'Thanks mate!'

'No problem. I know how much you love scoring in finals!'

Neymar Jr had learnt so much from playing with amazing players like Lionel, Luis and Andrés, and he was still learning every game. He wasn't quite the best in the world yet, but he was getting closer and closer to Lionel and Cristiano's level.

CHAPTER 23

BRAZILIAN SUCCESS

'What do you mean you're not playing in the Copa América?' Dani Alves asked. He was the Brazilian captain for the 2016 tournament and he was relying on Neymar Jr to be their star.

'I'm sorry!' Neymar Jr explained. 'Barcelona won't let me play in the Copa América *and* the Olympics. They said I had to choose and I chose the Olympics. I want to win that gold medal in front of the nation!'

Without Neymar Jr, the national team were knocked out by Peru in the first round. It was like the 2014 World Cup all over again.

'What a disaster!' Dani Alves told him when

they met up afterwards. 'Junior, we can't
even score goals without you, let alone win a
tournament.'

But even with Neymar Jr in the team, Brazil were
struggling to score goals. In their first two Olympic
matches, they drew 0–0 against both South Africa
and Iraq. Their fans had been dreaming of a glorious
home victory and they weren't happy at all. Neither
was Neymar Jr.

'What's happened to my shooting?' he complained
to his teammates. 'I've got to do better. I'm the
captain now and I've been scoring goals for
Barcelona all season!'

'Relax!' his young strike partners Gabriel Jesus and
Gabriel Barbosa told him. 'We're a team and we're
going to help you.'

In the third game, against Denmark, Douglas
Santos crossed from the left. Neymar Jr stretched
out his foot but he couldn't quite reach it. Luckily,
Gabriel Barbosa was there to score instead.

'Well done!' Neymar Jr cheered. Brazil were
finally off the mark at the Olympics and it was a

great relief. 'Now that we've got one goal, they're going to flood in!'

He was right. Gabriel Jesus, Luan and Gabriel Barbosa all scored to make it 4–0.

'That's more like it!' the coach Rogério Micale told his players in the dressing room after the match. But Neymar Jr still wasn't happy.

'The others are playing well but I'm not doing my job properly,' he told Micale.

'Your job is more than just scoring goals, Junior,' his coach told him. 'You're the team leader and you were involved in creating all of those goals. Don't be so hard on yourself.'

Neymar Jr nodded. There were plenty of matches left in the tournament for him to be a national hero. Against Colombia in the quarter-finals, Brazil won an early free-kick. It was a long way from goal but Neymar Jr stepped up and curled the ball right into the corner of the net.

Goooooooooooooooooooaaaaaaaaaaaaaaaaaaaaalllllllllll llllllllll!!!!!!!!!!!!!!!!

Neymar Jr was so pleased to be on the scoresheet at last. He pointed to the sky and jumped for joy.

'What a strike!' Luan shouted as the whole team celebrated together.

In the semi-finals, Neymar Jr tackled the Honduras centre back and lifted the ball over the goalkeeper. In the first minute of the match, he had made it 1–0 to Brazil. In the last minute of the match, he scored a penalty to make it 6–0.

'One goal in the quarter-final and then two goals in the semi-final. That means you should score a hat-trick in the final!' his teammate Marquinhos joked.

'No pressure, then!' Neymar Jr replied. The smile was back on his face.

In the final, Brazil faced Germany. It was the perfect opportunity to get revenge for that embarrassing 7–1 defeat at the 2014 World Cup. And this time, they had Neymar Jr in their team.

'I won't accept another silver medal,' he told Gabriel Jesus before the big match. 'Especially not when it would mean losing to Germany again!'

No, with nearly 60,000 Brazilians in the Maracanã Stadium, they had to win the gold. In the twenty-seventh minute, Neymar Jr scored another free-kick.

Gooooooooooooooooooooaaaaaaaaaaaaaaaallllllllllll llllllllllllll!!!!!!!!!!!!!!!!!

It was one of the best moments of his life as the stadium went wild and his teammates hugged him. But the match wasn't over yet. Germany equalised and it was still 1–1 after extra-time. The final would be decided on penalties.

'I'll take the last one,' Neymar Jr told Micale, just as he had told Scolari in the shoot-out against Chile at the World Cup two years earlier. He had been a hero that day – could he be a hero again?

As Neymar Jr made the long walk to the penalty spot, he knew this was his chance, the one that he had dreamed of since the age of three. It was the opportunity that Neymar Sr had dreamed of long before his son was even born.

'Come on, Junior!' he shouted from the stands. His crossed his fingers firmly and so did his grandson Davi next to him.

If Neymar Jr scored, Brazil would be Olympic Champions for the first time ever. He would be the hero, the captain and the star. He would

win something that not even Pelé had
achieved.

Neymar Jr kissed the ball, placed it down and
took the perfect spot-kick. The goalkeeper dived to
the right and his strike went high to the left. Brazil
had won the Olympic Gold! By the time the ball
hit the net, he was already in tears. It was the most
emotional moment of his life.

Once his tears had dried, it was carnival time.
Neymar Jr put on his favourite white headband for the
medal ceremony and pretended to bite into the precious
metal. His celebrations didn't end there. By the time he
returned to Spain, the Olympic rings had been tattooed
on his wrist and his hair was dyed blonde.

At the age of twenty-four, Neymar Jr had lived up
to his huge reputation as his country's next great
superstar. After his big move to Barcelona, many
Brazilians feared that he would forget about his
home. But they didn't need to worry. The smiles, the
skills, the dancing, the *ginga* rhythm, the incredible
natural footballing talent – Neymar Jr was 100 per
cent made in Brazil.

Turn the page for a special bonus
chapter of Neymar Jr's journey to
the World Cup. . .

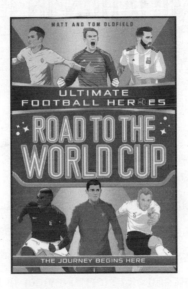

Chapter taken from *Road to the World Cup*
by Matt and Tom Oldfield
Available now!

PART ONE

HUMILIATION IN BELO HORIZONTE

Estádio Castelão, 4 July 2014

It was all going according to plan for Brazil at the 2014 World Cup. It wasn't their best team ever, but they had two very important weapons – the amazing home support and an in-form Neymar Jr. First Pelé, then Romário, then Ronaldo and Ronaldinho; now it was time for Brazil's latest superstar to shine. All hopes rested on Neymar Jr, the new Number 10.

'I want to win the World Cup,' he told the media before the tournament started, 'and this time, it will be right here in Brazil!'

Neymar Jr worked hard to make his dream come

true, scoring two goals against Croatia and two more against Cameroon. Brazil finished top of Group A, but the people demanded more. The excitement grew and grew all over the country. It was the only thing anyone talked about.

'Do you really think we can win our sixth World Cup?'

'If we've got Neymar Jr, we can beat anyone!'

In the knock-out rounds, the tournament got tougher, but Brazil kept pushing on towards glory. They beat Chile on penalties and with minutes to go, they were beating Colombia 2–1. Neymar Jr hadn't scored in either game, but he had helped set up all the goals. He was Brazil's main man and he was saving some magic for the semi-finals.

As Neymar Jr went to chest the ball down, a Colombian defender pushed his knee into his back. It seemed like a harmless, clumsy tackle, but it was a lot worse than it looked.

Owwwwwwwwwwwwww!

As play carried on, Neymar Jr fell to the floor, clutching his lower back and screaming with pain.

Worry spread like wildfire around the Estádio Castelão. Was Brazil's superstar badly injured? If so, what would they do without him?

Marcelo was the first to rush over to his friend and teammate. 'What happened?' he asked. 'Are you okay?'

'I don't know but I can't feel my legs!'

David Luiz was the next to arrive at the scene. He took one look at Neymar Jr's agony and called for help.

'Ref, stop the game!' he cried out. 'It's serious!'

As Neymar Jr left the pitch on a stretcher, he put a hand up to hide his tears. Was his tournament really over? He feared the worst. The Brazil supporters did too, but they still clapped and cheered. They needed him to get well as soon as possible. World Cup glory depended on it.

It wasn't good news. 'I'm afraid you've fractured one of the vertebrae in your back,' the team doctor told him.

Neymar Jr thought he knew the awful answer, but he had to ask. 'Is there any chance that I can play in the semi-final against Germany?'

The team doctor shook his head sadly.

'What about the final if we get there?' Neymar Jr asked.

The team doctor shook his head sadly once more. 'I'm sorry, but you need to rest for at least a month.'

The whole of Brazil was devastated, from the fans to the players. How could they continue without their superstar and leader?

It was the worst time of Neymar Jr's young life, but he put on a brave face. He had to stay positive, for the sake of the nation.

'It's a very difficult time for me,' he told the fans in a video, 'but the dream is not over yet. I'm confident that my teammates will win and become champions. We, the Brazilian people, will be celebrating soon!'

'You can win the World Cup without me,' he told his teammates. The atmosphere in the dressing room was as gloomy as a funeral. 'I'll be cheering you on!'

Neymar Jr couldn't cheer them on live at the Mineirão Stadium in Belo Horizonte, however. He needed to rest, and he knew it would be a nightmare to be so close to the pitch when he couldn't help his country.

Instead, Neymar Jr watched the game at home with his friends and family in São Paulo. It turned out to be the worst TV that Neymar Jr had ever seen. Brazil were 5–0 down after thirty minutes.

'That's it – I'm turning it off!' he shouted as Germany scored yet another goal in the second-half to make it 7–0.

It was too painful to watch any more. Without their superstar Number 10, Brazil had completely fallen apart. Where was the attacking flair? Germany's goalkeeper Manuel Neuer barely had to make a save. And where was the defending? It was their most humiliating defeat of all time.

Neymar Jr's 2014 World Cup dream was over. But the only way for Brazil to bounce back from despair was to look ahead. The future looked bright, as long as their leader was fit and firing.

'We have to move on,' Neymar Jr told his teammates. They were all still in shock. No-one dared to look at what the newspapers were saying about them. Would the country ever forgive them?

'Come on, the Road to the 2018 World Cup starts now!'

NEYMAR DA SILVA SANTOS
HONOURS

Santos

 Campeonato Paulista: 2010, 2011, 2012

 Copa do Brasil: 2010

 Copa Libertadores: 2011

 Recopa Sudamericana: 2012

Barcelona

 La Liga: 2014–15, 2015–16

 Copa del Rey: 2014–15, 2015–16

 Champions League: 2014–15

 FIFA Club World Cup: 2015

Brazil

 South American Youth Championship: 2011

 Olympic Silver Medal: 2012

🏆 FIFA Confederations Cup: 2013
🏆 Olympic Gold Medal: 2016

Individual

🏆 Brazilian Golden Ball: 2011
🏆 FIFA Puskás Award: 2011
🏆 South American Footballer of the Year: 2011, 2012
🏆 FIFA Confederations Cup Golden Ball: 2013
🏆 FIFA World Cup Bronze Boot: 2014
🏆 UEFA Champions League Team of the Season: 2014–15
🏆 FIFA FIFPro World XI: 2015

NEYMAR

11

THE FACTS

NAME: Neymar Da Silva Santos Júnior

DATE OF BIRTH: 5 February 1992

AGE: 26

PLACE OF BIRTH: Mogi das Cruzes, São Paulo

NATIONALITY: Brazil

BEST FRIEND: His dad, Neymar Sr.

CURRENT CLUB: Barcelona

POSITION: LW

THE STATS

Height (cm):	175
Club appearances:	410
Club goals:	240
Club trophies:	14
International appearances:	83
International goals:	53
International trophies:	2
Ballon d'Ors:	0

★ ★ ★ **HERO RATING: 91** ★ ★ ★

GREATEST MOMENTS

Type and search the web links to see the magic for yourself!

1 **27 JULY 2011,
ANTOS 4-5 FLAMENGO**

https://www.youtube.com/watch?v=olwF0yqAZFc
Neymar scored lots of amazing goals for his Brazilian club Santos but this is the best of them all. He was only nineteen when he tricked his way past two defenders, played a great one-two and then dribbled past another defender before lifting the ball over the diving goalkeeper. This wonder goal won The FIFA Puskás Award for best goal of the year.

2 30 JUNE 2013,
BRAZIL 3-0 SPAIN

https://www.youtube.com/watch?v=t-rI2RST_CY
In the Confederations Cup Final, Brazil faced the
European and World Champions, Spain. It was the
biggest game of his career so far and so Neymar put
on a match-winning display. He scored a brilliant
goal and played so well that Gerard Piqué got sent off
trying to tackle him. This was a very proud moment
for Neymar and a sign of things to come.

3 26 OCTOBER 2013,
BARCELONA 2-1 REAL MADRID

https://www.youtube.com/watch?v=dVu51otWbLE
This was Neymar's first ever *El Clásico* match but
he didn't show it. With nearly 100,000 supporters
watching him in the Nou Camp, he scored the first
goal and then set up Alexis Sánchez's winner with a
brilliant pass. If the Barcelona fans didn't already love
their big new signing, they certainly did after this.

★ 4   6 JUNE 2015, BARCELONA 3-1 JUVENTUS

https://www.youtube.com/watch?v=1mVu7AzvCDo
Neymar took his first ever Champions League
final in his stride. He helped Ivan Rakiti to score
Barcelona's first goal and then combined with Lionel
Messi and Luis Suárez to score the third himself.
It was a special way to end a special night. 'MSN',
Barcelona's superstar strikeforce, was on fire.

★ 5   20 AUGUST 2016, BRAZIL 1-1 GERMANY (5-4 ON PENALTIES)

https://www.youtube.com/watch?v=vGl26eScJKc
After the embarrassing defeat at the 2014 World
Cup, this was the perfect chance for Brazil to get
their revenge on Germany and win another major
trophy. With the pressure of the nation on him,
Neymar captained his country to glory. Not only did
he score an amazing free-kick but he also scored the
winning penalty in the shoot-out.

PLAY LIKE YOUR HEROES

THE NEYMAR FLICK

SEE IT HERE **You Tube**

https://www.youtube.com/watch?v=xh30o43qmQM

STEP 1: Wait for a defender to charge towards you.

STEP 2: Get the front of your foot under the ball and at the perfect moment, flick it up in the air.

STEP 3: Don't put too much power or height on the flick. You want it to go just over the defender's head and then land the other side.

STEP 4: Dodge the defender, who may well try to foul you for trying such outrageous skills.

STEP 5: Run onto the ball and bring it down with perfect control.

STEP 6: If you're a real entertainer, flick the ball back over the defender's head.

STEP 7: Once you're bored of that trick, move on to some step-overs or even a rainbow flick.

TEST YOUR KNOWLEDGE

QUESTIONS

1. How did Neymar have a lucky escape when he was a baby?

2. What did Neymar give to his teammates at Gremetal?

3. How old was Neymar when he joined Santos?

4. Which Spanish club tried to sign Neymar first and how old was he?

5. What are Neymar's fans called in Brazil?

6. Who was Neymar's childhood hero, who he then played with at Santos?

7. Neymar scored on his Brazil debut – true or false?

8. When and where did Neymar first meet Lionel Messi?

9. Which Barcelona manager signed Neymar and how much did they pay for him?

10. Who joined Barcelona first – Neymar or Luis Suárez?

11. What number does Neymar wear for Brazil and who else famously wore that shirt?

Answers below. . . No cheating!

11. He wears Number 10, just like Pelé.
10. Neymar. Neymar joined in 2013 and Suárez joined in 2014.
Martino was the manager and Neymar cost Barcelona about £72million
7. True 8. At the 2011 FIFA World Club Cup in Japan. 9. Gerardo
Madrid tried to sign him when he was 13 5. Neymarzetes 6. Robinho
1. He survived a serious car crash. 2. White headbands 3. 11 4. Real

This summer, your favourite football heroes will pull on their country's colours to go head-to-head for the ultimate prize – the World Cup.

Celebrate by making sure you have six of the best Ultimate Football Heroes, now with limited-edition international covers!

COMING 31ST MAY

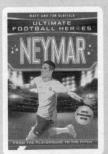

FOLLOW IN THE FOOTSTEPS OF LEGENDS. . .

Bridge the gap between past and present by stepping into the shoes of six classic World Cup heroes and reading their exciting stories – from the playground to the pitch, and to superstardom!

COMING 31ST MAY